Chi

The Evolution a

Knives, Sw
A World History of Edged Weapon Warfare

by Martina Sprague

RUSTPROOFING — 36

Copyright 2013 Martina Sprague

All rights reserved. No part of this book may be reproduced in any form or by any means, electronic or otherwise, without the prior written consent of the author.

Acknowledgements:

Front cover image pictures Chinese swords of the Sui Dynasty, found near Luoyang. Image source: Uploadalt, reproduced under Wikimedia Commons license.

Back cover image pictures the legendary sword-making master, Ou Yezi, of the Spring and Autumn period. Image source: Leong0083, reproduced under Wikimedia Commons license.

Image source for horse logo (slightly adapted) on back cover: CoralieM Photographie, reproduced under Wikimedia Commons license.

TABLE OF CONTENTS

Some Notes about the Knives, Swords, and Bayonets Series	4
Introduction	10
The Sword in the Eastern Zhou Dynasty (770-256 BCE)	17
The Sword in the Qin and Han Dynasties (221 BCE-220 CE)	36
The Sword in the Three Kingdoms Period (220-263 CE)	42
The Sword in the Sui Dynasty (581-618 CE)	48
The Sword in the Tang and Song Dynasties (618-1279 CE)	53
The Sword in the Ming and Qing Dynasties (1368-1912 CE)	59
Concluding Remarks	69
Notes	74
Bibliography	96

SOME NOTES ABOUT THE KNIVES, SWORDS, AND BAYONETS SERIES

Knives, Swords, and Bayonets: A World History of Edged Weapon Warfare is a series of books that examines the history of edged weapons in Europe, Asia, Africa, the Americas, and the Middle East and surrounding areas before gunpowder increased the distance between combatants. Edged weapons were developed to function in foot or mounted combat. The primary battlefield function often determined the specific design of the weapon. In poorer societies the general populace frequently modified agricultural tools into weapons of war. The techniques for employing these tools in civilian life translated into viable methods of combat. When the advent of firearms made certain edged weapons obsolete, close range combat continued to rely on foot soldiers carrying knives and bayonets as sidearms to modern artillery weapons. But even in ancient times edged weapons were seldom the primary arms, but were frequently employed as sidearms to long range projectiles. Rebel fighters of Third World countries have likewise used edged weapons extensively in near modern and modern wars.

The Knives, Swords, and Bayonets series of books takes a critical look at the relationship between the soldier, his weapon, and the social and political mores of the times. Each book examines the historical background and metallurgic science of the knife, sword, or bayonet respectively, and explores the handling characteristics and combat applications of each weapon. The author suggests that the reader make specific note of how battlefield need and geography influenced the design of the weapon, the type of warfare employed (guerrilla, rebellion, chivalry, pitched battle, skirmishes, mass armies, etc.), and the type of armor available to counter the blow of a knife or sword.

The historical treatment of edged weaponry could fill volumes. Because of the vastness of the subject, certain restrictive measures had to be applied in order to keep the series within a reasonable length while still giving adequate coverage. For example, the author has chosen to cover Chinese and Japanese but not Korean sword history. Every reader is thus bound to find some favorite details omitted. While many treatments of the subject focus exclusively on the technological aspects of weapons, this series also considers the political climate and the environmental or geographical factors under which the weapons evolved. Moreover, every culture, western or non-western, employs a number of subtleties that are exceedingly difficult to understand fully, unless one has spent time living in and studying the specific culture. The same can be said for every subculture (a culture within a culture), such as a military organization. The reader is reminded that, unlike science which is mathematically precise, history offers a broad range of perspectives on every issue.

The narrative the author has chosen to write portrays the development and dynamics of edged weaponry from ancient to modern times, including the soldier's training and his view of military service. The close relationship between military and political or social history also spurred the author's desire to examine the carry of edged weapons as symbols of military rank and social status. Rather than covering battles in their entirety, the author has elected to illustrate bits and pieces of particular battles that exemplify how the weapon in question was used. The book series comprises ten books arranged by weapon type, geographical area, or time period, and is designed to introduce the reader to the great assortment of edged weaponry that has been used with varied success in most regions of the world. Each book in the series is an entity in itself. In other words, it is not necessary to read the books in any particular order. Hopefully, the series will provide the reader with a solid foundation for continued study.

For her research, and in order to render an analysis that closely describes the dynamics of battle and the cultural aspects surrounding edged weaponry, the author has relied on a large number of primary and secondary source materials including historical treatises, artifacts located at museums, ancient artists' renditions of war in sculpture, paint, and poem, eyewitness accounts to the events in question, books, articles, documentaries, Internet resources, university lectures, personal correspondence, and direct hands-on practice with weapons in mock battles. Note that source material is often contradictory in nature. For example, swordsmen of the same era and geographical region frequently differed in their views with respect to the conduct of battle or the "best" type of sword or battlefield technique. The reader is encouraged to keep an open mind and consider the different possibilities that the soldier faced, and why he would emphasize a particular type of weapon or combat technique over another. The endnotes provide additional information, clarification, and exceptions to commonly propagated historical beliefs.

The author reminds the reader that despite their lethal features, edged weapons are not randomly chosen bars of steel that can cut and kill. The difference between victory and defeat often lies in the soldier's knowledge, skill, and fortitude; in how well he handles his weapon, but also in how well the weapon adheres to the laws of physics with respect to balance and motion. Studying metallurgic science is the key to understanding the relationship between the weapon smith and the soldier. The knife- or swordsmith thus carried part of the responsibility for the soldier's success or failure. Additionally, edged weapons were an integral part of the soldier's kit and often represented abstract qualities such as bravery and honor. By understanding the history of knives, swords, and bayonets, one will gain insight into the culture—the external and internal forces—that shaped the men who relied on these weapons in personal struggles of life and death.

Chinese Swords

Chinese Swords

The Evolution and Use of the Jian and Dao

INTRODUCTION

Edged weapons became a mainstay in early Chinese history and through the Ming (1368-1644 CE) and Qing (1644-1912 CE) dynasties. The Chinese used swords to settle personal disputes, win military battles, and indicate one's social and martial status through the end of the Imperial Period. "Qing rulers could be quite pragmatic about the bearing of arms by the general populace: for instance, the Kangxi emperor was known to have vetoed a request by an official to disarm the people of Shandong Province."[2]

China, a country of vast resources, developed its metal and iron industry earlier than its western counterparts and achieved great advances in metallurgic science. There were two classes of Chinese swords: the straight double edged *jian* and the slightly curved single edged *dao*. The jian was an extraordinary weapon that transcended time; its history spanning more than three thousand years. The distinguishing characteristics of the jian were its straight shape and double cutting edge. The edge, which was exceptionally sharp at the tip and approximately six inches down the blade, gave the swordsman the advantage of reach. An attack with the jian could be very subtle and still cause significant damage, particularly to the ligaments in an opponent's sword hand or arm. By contrast, the six inches of the blade nearest the hilt were blunt and strong, and could be used effectively as defense against an incoming attack. The hand guard was typically decorated, the handle made of hardwood and wrapped in animal skin in order to provide comfort and a good grip. A tassel, which purpose it was to provide balance to the blade, was attached to the end of the handle. The tassel could also take the shape of a rope that the swordsman could wrap around his wrist, thereby gaining the ability to extend his reach an additional few inches by throwing the sword toward his opponent and retrieving it quickly. The sheath like the hand guard was typically ornamented and displayed the status of the sword's owner.[3]

The jian proved effective mainly for chivalry combat in the Zhou Dynasty (1045-256 BCE), and was later carried by the nobility as a symbol of status. Military officers, perhaps because of their association with the nobility, seem to have preferred the double edged jian over the dao. While the successful use of the jian required flexibility in the grip and the ability to move with the forces the swordsman encountered in combat, it also required a stable foundation. The general populace's use of this sword for the perfection of character and the attainment of health reflected the revered nature of the weapon.

The single edged dao, by contrast, was issued to the rank and file. The distinguishing characteristics of the dao were its curved shape and singe cutting edge. The sword had no set curve or length but came in several shapes. Some dao were long and others short; some were broad and resembled the European sabers. The dao proved useful mainly in cavalry combat, which started to gain popularity in the Western Han Dynasty (202 BCE-9 CE). The dao was a true soldier's weapon that required more attention to fighting skill than finesse. The slashing movements employed by the dao-wielding swordsman proved practical from horseback, and were capable of producing impressive momentum and cutting power through the uninterrupted circular flow of the blade.[4] Variations of the dao started to see use several hundred years prior to the unification of the empire in 221 BCE. For example, a shorter version of the dao was used also in walking infantry. The first dao were made of bronze. By the third century BCE, iron and steel became the preferred materials used in weapons production.

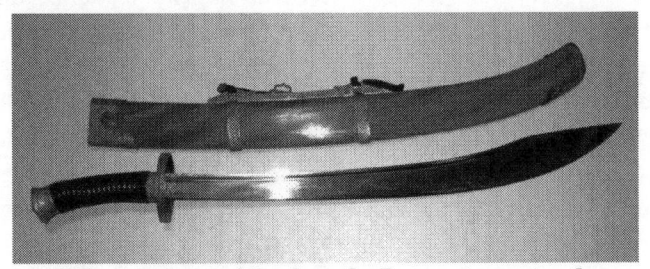

Chinese dao with sheath. In contrast to the straight jian, the broad-bladed and curved dao proved a practical battlefield weapon and was well-suited for mounted combat. Image source: Lawrence Kane.

In comparison to the attention enjoyed by the Japanese samurai, Chinese swords and swordsmen have been given relatively little focus in written sources, despite evidence that reveal that Japanese swords developed from the basics of Chinese forging and tempering techniques and arrived in Japan around the seventh century CE. The lack of attention afforded Chinese combat swords is due in part to the long history of the sword in China. Neither the jian nor the dao, both of which were developed during the

Bronze Age, were considered revolutionary "new" technology.[5] Moreover, the sword, although used alongside of other combat arms—mainly the bow, which "remained the predominant tactical weapon of field armies through the [sixteenth] century"—never became the distinctive weapon of choice. The Chinese expression, "The Five Weapons," referred to bows, sticks, spears, pikes, and halberds, but not swords.[6] Confucian values also influenced how one tended to view things of a military nature, and literary interests often took precedence over military matters. Furthermore, the transition to Manchu rule in the seventeenth century CE may have had a negative effect on scholastic interests in arms. When firearms became more accurate in the nineteenth century CE, swordsmanship for the purpose of combat became less common and people started training with the sword mainly for the attainment of health. The sword, however, continued to be carried as a symbol of status and was used occasionally in battle as late as the 1930s.[7]

Although the Qing Dynasty censored and restricted the access to military treatises, written records did exist due to the need to educate the primarily Han Chinese troops. "A survey of technical and artistic treatises reveals a considerable number of works dealing with steel bladed swords, published as early as the [fourth century CE]."[8] Examples of such written works include *Yue Nu Jian* from the Spring and Autumn period (722-481 BCE) and *Jian Dao* from the Western Han Dynasty (202 BCE-9 CE).[9] Difficulties with the interpretation of said material emerge, however, through the observation that the authors of the Chinese texts were generally not practicing soldiers. Military matters were often performed by others than the educated elite who considered themselves too "civil" for leading the troops in battle, and the view that the literati held of warfare changed several times throughout the long history of Imperial China. As anti-militarism grew during the Song Dynasty (960-1279 CE), civil officials continued to separate themselves from warfare. Rather than participating in battle they exercised their military responsibilities by giving orders to military officials, and generally blamed China's problems on the standing armies.[10]

The existing Chinese literature available to students in the West is limited and can be divided into three main groups: ancient Confucian and Daoist treatments and poetry, military studies of warfare and strategic thought with a key focus on deception, and modern books written primarily for the sports/martial arts interested person. While Confucian and Daoist thought and poetry underpinned the development of China's military history, these sources are often difficult to understand by students in the West and can be interpreted in several ways. Military studies, such as the *Seven Military Classics of Ancient China*, differ from Confucianism by elevating the military sphere and emphasizing the timeless principles of strategy.[11] However, the Classics fail to consider the technical uses of the sword and the skill of the swordsman. Moreover, since much of China's military history revolves around internal conflicts, Sunzi's (also known as Sun-tzu) *Art of War*, for example, assumes a Chinese opponent and pays little attention to the problems associated with the nomads and other mounted warriors.[12] By contrast, the modern martial arts books focus on the practical uses of the sword but tend to neglect history. Or they give only a very sketchy account of the philosophical and military factors that influenced the development of swords and swordsmanship. Artifacts uncovered in tombs and other archaeological sites are also available for study, and are housed at museums in Asia, the Middle East, and the Western world. These artifacts provide information mainly about metallurgic science.

The actual usage of swords must thus be discerned by studying the shapes of the blades and the physical principles that apply to swordsmanship, and by making certain inferences based on the history of Chinese civil and military culture. Note that although documents located at the Chinese National Palace Museum and in databases containing historical Chinese texts frequently do not exist in translation, ancient drawings and other artwork can be viewed at a variety of museums and tend to reveal some of the movements and tactics the swordsman used. Based on an examination of these sources, however, it becomes apparent that, in contrast to Japanese swords which were (and are) considered treasures, virtually no literature exists in the West that balances the philosophy and history of Chinese swords with the technical uses of the sword by mass armies and swordsmen engaged in single combat.[13] This book hopes to provide that balance by examining the functionality of the jian and dao, and by placing the development of swords and swordsmanship in China in an easily understood historical context.

China has a rich and complex history originating in the Neolithic Period (5500-3000 BCE).

Although China's culture was far from static, this book is limited to those dynasties in which significant changes to the development of the sword occurred. The Eastern Zhou Dynasty (770-256 BCE) laid the foundation for the evolution of metallurgic science, philosophical thought, and swordsmanship and will therefore receive slightly greater treatment than subsequent periods. By contrast, not much focus will be placed on the three centuries following the Three Kingdoms period (220-263 CE) until the emergence of the Sui Dynasty (581-618 CE). Albeit a turbulent era, this period saw few new developments in sword design. The most noteworthy military innovation may have been the appearance of stirrups, which benefited the mounted warrior. New developments to the sword took place when swords began to migrate across Asia during the Tang Dynasty (618-907 CE). Further improvements occurred in the late eleventh century CE, when Song infantry troops needed a new weapon in response to heavily armored cavalry riders. The Ming and Qing Dynasties (1368-1912 CE) saw considerable experimentation in sword design. The saber grew in importance and was carried by cavalrymen and foot soldiers alike. Craftsmanship reached new heights and regulation swords were constructed for the purpose of upholding the social order in China's highly bureaucratic society. This book thus follows a chronological path through China's dynasties.[14] The concluding remarks recap the long history of sword design and swordsmanship in China, with focus on the philosophical value one assigned the sword.

THE SWORD IN THE EASTERN ZHOU DYNASTY (770-256 BCE)

China's dynasties were established through wars. Rebellions and dynastic declines often followed periods of warfare. The country had the assets to support military action through a large population and natural resources, such as iron. In early history, the tactics of warfare developed "around the most efficient use of bladed weapons . . . for both the individual and the organized unit."[15] A small bronze knife dating to around 3000 BCE found in northwestern China, is one of the earliest metal weapons/tools that archaeologists have uncovered. Daggers and swords dating to around 800 BCE have also been unearthed at several archaeological sites, along with more than 140 iron objects dating to earlier than the fifth century BCE.[16] The short tanged sword (a tang is an extension of the blade running through the handle) dating to around the sixth century BCE developed from the tanged dagger. The Chinese seem to have invented these kinds of swords independently of western inventions, although some features such as a slight "taper of the blade in the lower third of its length" can be found also in "late Bronze Age swords in Europe west of the Alps."[17] Although the "Mesopotamian bronze culture of the fourth millennium [BCE] antedates the earliest [bronze culture] of which we have knowledge in China by some 2,000 years," and the former was "instrumental in the rise of China's bronze industry," the archaeological finds unearthed in China demonstrate that the Chinese people concerned themselves with the use of edged weaponry through most of their history.[18]

The necessity to survive in armed combat facilitated the search for and development of better materials. Bronze metallurgy proved useful for the construction of tools (an economic necessity) and weapons (a military necessity), and spread rapidly from one end of Asia to another.[19] Prior to the Eastern Zhou Dynasty, martiality and civility held equal weight with respect to conflict resolution. Whether one relied on *wu* (martial) or *wen* (civil) depended on the likelihood that one of these concepts would preserve the state's "awesomeness."[20] In the Eastern Zhou Dynasty, the nobility dominated weapon production.[21] Many of the smaller states became united through conquest and colonization. As the dynastic territory grew, philosophers such as Confucius and Laozi, founders of Confucianism and Daoism, came to affect Chinese thought and ethics including the development of swordsmanship.[22] Although swordsmanship originated as a result of battlefield needs, social, ethical, and political considerations influenced the shapes and uses of the sword. For example, all kinds of people including Daoist priests and those training to become warriors carried the jian. The affection afforded the straight sword, also among the part of the population not directly exposed to armed conflict, indicates the value one placed on this weapon.

The blade of the jian tapers to a sharp point, which made it particularly well-suited for precision thrusts to specific targets. Image source: Nazanian, reproduced under Wikimedia Commons license.

Some jian had decorative hilts that indicated the status of the bearer and the value and respect he afforded the weapon. The characters on this sword state that the weapon was made and used by the King Gou Jian of Yue, who reigned 496-465 BCE near the end of the Spring and Autumn Period. Image source: Yutwong, reproduced under Wikimedia Commons license.

Along with the concept of the Mandate of Heaven, which allowed Chinese society to establish its political legitimacy, came a feudal social order with the nobility owning the farming land and allocating it to the serfs.[23] By the time of the Spring and Autumn period, the strength of the feudal lords had overcome the weaker kings. As a result of instability and weakened prestige in royal circles, chivalry preceded by rituals took precedence over infantry battles.[24] Wars should have a moral legitimacy, it was reasoned; they should be ethical and righteous.[25] The warrior should be brave without appearing heroic; he should display modesty and demonstrate composure under pressure.

Militarism in the period was expressed through the war chariot, an offensive form of military transportation that worked best in connection with long-reaching weapons, such as bows. Horseback riding was also introduced. The sword, by contrast, was mainly a close combat weapon. Chariots and cavalry, however, were of limited use against infantry, because horses frequently refused to overrun walking infantry or hurl themselves against sharp weapons. These limitations demonstrate some of the difficulties the Chinese experienced in early warfare, before the stirrup emerged as an important invention that promoted efficiency with respect to wielding swords and other weapons from horseback. Although the long and straight jian proved efficient for combat in the early Eastern Zhou Dynasty, and despite advances in metallurgic science, the shorter dagger-type jian continued to remain popular in infantry units.[26]

At the conclusion of battle, the victors absorbed the defeated enemy's weapons and copied new technology. The outcome of prior battles helped determine the degree of refinement that took place, and helped direct the evolution of metallurgic science. How different cultures developed and applied bladed weapons also depended on the geography of the country and the material resources available. Early jian were made of bronze, an alloy of copper and tin;

however, bronze was quite heavy, which limited the length of the sword. By the late Spring and Autumn period, the Chinese constructed well-developed non-laminated bronze swords. Some of these swords utilized a higher tin content in the cutting edges than in the center of the blade. By lowering the percentage of tin in the center, this part of the sword could be made more flexible. By contrast, the high tin content in the edges gave the sword sharpness and the ability to cut through armor, or to sever a limb or head from an opponent's body. A sword also had to be resilient and strong enough to function in a defensive manner involving blocks and parries against an opponent's weapon. By examining the technical developments in the metallurgy of combat swords, one can discern a clear relationship between battlefield needs and the search for natural resources that were used in the construction of edged weaponry.

Although bronze and copper were originally used in the construction of weapons, tools, and ornaments, access to natural resources and the ability to mine iron gave China an advantage over other cultures with access only to bronze.[27] Decarbonized cast iron and steel swords appeared in China as early as the middle of the fifth century BCE. Around 300 BCE, as a result of a shift toward greater military forces and larger armies, the Chinese started to use iron in weapons on a regular basis.[28] The widespread use of iron led to the production of stronger weapons displaying a greater variety in style and blade size. As metallurgic science improved, the weight of the sword could be decreased and strength and flexibility increased. The length of the sword was thus gradually extended. A typical bronze sword from the early

Warring States period (453-221 BCE) measured around 32 inches in length. By contrast, a steel sword from the later part of this period could measure a full 55 inches in length and needed two hands to wield successfully.[29] A sword that was too long and flexible would be useless, however, or at least dangerous to use as a weapon of defense against an opponent's sword or other close combat weapon, such as a halberd. A sword that was so flexible that it had movement in the tip when thrust at specific targets would also complicate the swordsman's accuracy with the weapon. In order to achieve a high quality sword that served the dual purpose of sharpness and flexibility, the swordsmith relied on composites of various types of steel, with alternating layers of hard and soft steel. The use of laminates which could flex under stress and return to their original shape proved an important evolutionary step in the sword making process.[30]

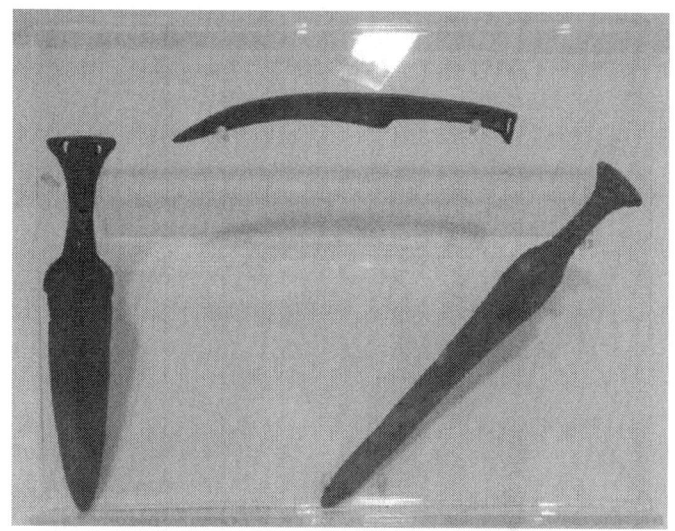

Two straight bronze swords and a curved bronze knife from the Warring States period. Image source: Daderot, Yunnan Provincial Museum, reproduced under Wikimedia Commons license.

To solve the problems associated with crafting a sword that could be used both offensively and defensively against a variety of weapons, one needed a skilled swordsmith. Jian swordsmiths were highly respected in Chinese society, and had likely worked on refining their craft for most of their lives:

> The man who forged swords for the Minister of War was eighty years of age. Yet he never made the slightest slip in his work. The Minister of War said to him, "Is it your skill, Sir, or have you any method?" "It is concentration," replied the man. "When twenty years old, I took to

forging swords. I cared for nothing else. If a thing was not a sword, I did not notice it. I availed myself of whatever energy I did not use in other directions in order to secure greater efficiency in the direction required."[31]

In addition to skill in the factors relating to metallurgic science, the swordsmith needed a good understanding of the finer details of swordsmanship and of the battlefield situation in which the swordsman might find himself. For example, to produce an efficient sword that was properly balanced and would serve the intended purpose, the swordsmith needed knowledge of how the length of the sword affected combat efficiency. Infantry swords, for example, were normally shorter than swords wielded from horseback. A good sword could "rip through iron as if it were mud."[32] The straight shape of the jian also commanded a high degree of accuracy in thrusting attacks to precise targets, such as the throat, armpit, or heart. This consideration made it difficult to attain expertise with the weapon. If the thrust lacked the necessary precision; for example, because the blade was too long or too flimsy, not only might the swordsman miss the target, the tip of the sword might break upon impact with the opponent's armor. If missing the target entirely, the swordsman would be in a vulnerable position while giving his opponent an opportune moment to counterattack.[33] Thus the life of the swordsman rested in part in the hands of the swordsmith, who had to have an intuitive understanding of the rigors of battle and the dangers and difficulties the swordsman would face.

Moreover, since Confucian and Daoist philosophical concepts such as *yin* and *yang* (the balance of forces) dominated the period, the swordsmith had to be "in tune" with the more elusive cultural beliefs of Chinese society, as noted in a description of Ganjiang, a legendary swordsmith of the Warring States period:

> To make the swords, Ganjiang collected the iron essence of the Five Mountains, and the metal efflorescence of the Valleys of Six Unions. He attended upon Heaven and waited upon Earth; Yin and Yang shone together; the Hundred Spirits approached and observed; the *qi* of heaven descended . . .[34]

Sword making and sword practice thus took skill and character, and cultivated an inner quality in each person who chose to engage in such matters. Originating in "the nation's spiritual strength residing between heaven and earth," sword practice became a means of "outward-directed expression of what lies inside."[35] It emphasized philosophical and intangible aspects, such as calmness and correctness. For example, crude techniques used in fighting resulted in clashing energies with one's opponent, and were considered inefficient: "Strong contact with both weapons [created] double-weightedness, a condition that . . . [violated] the yin and yang . . . because both weapons [were] exerting yang force simultaneously."[36]

By contrast, the subtle manipulation of the sword cultivated the mind and the spirit, allowing the intrinsic energy to lead the physical body in battle.[37] The swordsman's grip should be firm enough to deliver a blow with power, but flexible enough to keep the sword fluid during attack, defense, and counterattack. A highly skilled practitioner was able to direct the sword to the target, using subtle moves in his fingers and wrist that required minimum force, until it appeared as though he used only his mind to guide the sword.[38] The thumb and middle finger were used for flexibility in guiding the sword, and the other fingers were used when the situation mandated a sturdier grip.[39] Such accomplishments were possible only if one had practiced with the sword until it came to feel as a part of one's body. For example, the sword hand must be properly aligned, or one risked breaking the thumb or having the sword twisted out of one's hand upon impact with the opponent's weapon.

Power and flexibility were also evident in the swordsman's stance. A good stance provided lateral stability and allowed the swordsman to intercept and counter strikes from the front and side. The pommel constituted a secondary weapon that could be used to halt the advance of an opponent approaching from the rear. For example, a strike with the pommel to the head or throat of an adversary to the rear might buy one enough time to decapitate or dismember a second opponent approaching from the front or side. Such maneuvers against more than one adversary required excellent timing as well as precision. An examination of the difficulties associated with "proper" sword practice demonstrates why the jian came to be viewed as one of the most revered of Chinese weapons: It had a long and unbroken history and reflected Chinese culture, values, and warrior spirit. "Its use required resourcefulness, adaptability, and cleverness within the speed and power of its movements."[40]

When the Zhou started to disintegrate and conflicts became more common, other ideas began to gain hold. Disputes between states resulted in full-scale warfare, and *wu* became the driving force behind conquest.[41] When the Chinese philosopher Confucius died in 479 BCE, more practical methods of warfare took the place of the Confucian ideals. The Warring States period began with the destruction and tripartition of the powerful state of Jin, and is characterized by new military reforms and the end of the chariot system of warfare. As expressed in Sunzi's *Art of War*, battle philosophy emphasized winning. The tactics of trickery and deception were elevated and described as virtues of great generals.[42] Sunzi did not speak of a mutually agreed upon code of conduct. Rather, he assessed the terrain, weather, and leadership for the purpose of determining if the conditions favored victory. New weapons were developed as a result of the need to meet the greater brutality of the period. Cavalry was one of them. Infantry, however, remained an important part of the armies.[43]

This bamboo book of Sunzi's *Art of War* was either commissioned or transcribed by the Qianlong Emperor (1711-1799 CE). Image source: vlasta2, reproduced under Wikimedia Commons license.

As weapons started to see mass production with the unification of the empire toward the end of the third century BCE, swords became plainer and were primarily made of iron rather than bronze.[44] Infantrymen carried iron swords along with spears and crossbows.[45] The mining industry grew. Assyrians worked Asian mines for copper, lead, and iron. As indicated by one observer, "Upon the Steppes of Tartary, and in the wildest parts of Siberia, the remains of old copper-furnaces, small and of rude construction are met with."[46] Artifacts that have been unearthed indicate that the Chinese had considerable knowledge of metallurgic science, and were in possession of sophisticated methods of sword making. Iron, which had almost twice the melting point of bronze, was a difficult metal to refine and blend with carbon to make steel. Several grades of iron and steel had to be combined in order to make a battle-worthy sword. Iron therefore proved a highly precious commodity. Moreover, a combat blade might have different attributes, some of which enhanced the sword's performance and some of which hindered it. For example, while soft-grade steel had good shock absorbing qualities, hard-grade steel could hold an edge better. Through the technique of pattern welding, which involved the folding and twisting of several pieces of steel of different qualities, the carbon could be evenly distributed throughout the blade.[47]

Other techniques used in sword making involved sandwiching larger plates of different types of steel, referred to as multi-plate construction. This technique, which the Chinese had been using since the Bronze Age, was eventually transferred from the Chinese mainland to Japan. "Trade and conquest not only spread sword making technologies, but also the style and use of swords. Cross-pollination of sword forms was more the rule than the exception." The Chinese were also the first to develop the idea "to use clay to achieve different levels of hardness in the edge and the back" of the blade. The use of clay proved effective, because it allowed the blade to cool at different rates. For example, the body of the blade was covered in clay and would cool slower than the edges which were bare. The edges would thus "form a harder crystalline form of steel," while the body would form a softer steel. The value of this type of sword making lay in the dual characteristics required of a good battle blade: It had to be hard enough to hold an edge well, yet soft enough at the core to give it flexibility and shock absorbing qualities.[48] While the edge must be able to cut through whatever type of armor one were likely to encounter on the battlefield, it must also be resilient and strong enough to function in a defensive manner involving blocks and parries against an opponent's weapon. Moreover, when thrusting into a specific target, the blade must remain straight for accuracy. A blade that could flex properly would return to its original shape after flexing.

When the Japanese started imitating the curved shape of the Chinese sabers, they adopted the use of clay in sword construction as well. The migration of Chinese swords and sword making skills to Japan further demonstrates that Chinese weapons production was envied by other countries, who came to rely on Chinese swords to meet their own battlefield needs. The "form of the [s]word [was] determined by the duty expected of it," and the shape of the sword directly influenced the weapon's effectiveness in combat. This concept held true regardless of specific cultural traits. The sword had three main uses: cutting, thrusting, and guarding. Since each requisite interfered to some extent with the other, various modifications had to be adopted. For example, men of inferior strength and stature would rely on a curved blade, because a straight blade required great strength to wield in order to inflict a deep cut. Moreover, the curved blade had superior cutting capabilities because it was always presented obliquely, or at an acute angle to the target. Although a slash that followed a curved path would take longer to launch against its own inertia, it had the potential to build sufficient momentum for severing limbs. This factor contributed to the efficiency of the nomads, who were fighting from horseback.[49] By contrast, a thrust with a straight sword had an advantage in time and reach. Additionally, a thrust, which could reach the vital parts of the body unprotected by bones and armor, often proved fatal even with only a few inches' penetration.[50]

Fighting with the sword followed a straightforward approach. After the first deflection, the counter-cut was aimed at a disabling target such as the forearm. The next series of cuts allowed the swordsman to move forward without risk of taking a cut. This was possible because the opponent had been rendered harmless by the forearm cut and could not grasp his weapon. The series of cuts that followed were aimed at killing the adversary by severing a major limb or the head from the body, or by thrusting the weapon into his heart.[51] This deeply penetrating thrust involving the first third of the blade could also be aimed at the throat, midsection, or leg.[52] Another tactic was to dodge and intercept the attack by slashing off the opponent's wrist or forearm. Considered both useful and noble, this type of maneuver would neutralize the threat while sparing the adversary his life. Jian techniques, however, typically involved small and effortless movements. A chop with the blade required a large movement and considerable effort, and was normally not the preferred technique. To reach success with a technique that required finesse, the swordsman must remain calm and wait until the opponent had committed himself to the attack.[53]

The swordsman would also use the jian to defend against long spears or staffs. Knowledge of the enemy's weapons would help one determine the most suitable type of defense and counterattack. For example, since a spear was normally thrust straight forward, the swordsman might try to dodge the attack and move to close range where he could reach his opponent with the sword.[54] Naturally, such a maneuver required timing and skill at footwork which provided movement forward, back, and to the side, enabling one to control the fight and redirecting the motion of the opponent's sword.[55] For example, when faced with overhead attacks or downward chops, footwork could be used to step slightly to the side of the attack while countering with a strike into the opponent's armpit. This evasive maneuver and counter-cut could also be employed against an aggressive opponent who displayed his techniques from a distance. If facing a particularly aggressive opponent one might choose to rely on the opponent's momentum by stepping back, luring him to step forward, and thrusting the tip of the sword into his body. Control of the opponent's weapon could also be achieved by establishing contact with the blade and pressing against his weapon. Such a move was used as an intermediary or transitioning technique. In other words, it was not an end in itself.[56] All controlling and deflecting techniques and counter-cuts required good timing and the ability to transition from defense to offense smoothly without halting the sword's momentum.

Although the length of the sword increased in the late Warring States period, the practical length of jian varied only somewhat in order to accommodate the stature of the wielder. Ultimately, the right length was a matter of feel and depended on the practitioner's personal taste and skill. A guideline when choosing a sword was to grasp the handle, stand with the arm along one's side, and hold the sword vertically along the outside of one's arm with the tip pointing up. Ideally the tip should be level with the swordsman's ear.[57] Despite these guidelines, the philosopher Zhuangzi suggested around 300 BCE that it mattered little whether one chose to fight with a short or a long sword. Rather, the best way to use a sword was to "make an empty feint. Then open your opponent by giving him an obvious advantage. Then strike, and get there first." Zhuangzi also emphasized training with the sword for health and as a "way of life" for the peasants. He recorded that martial arts training that included sword practice had made life prosperous among the population: The middle part of the "Sword of the Feudal Lord" supposedly harmonized "with the song in the hearts of the people, bringing peace to every village."[58] Zhuangzi's work reflects the Daoist philosophical and religious tradition of self-cultivation. Zhuangzi believed that the process of nature unified all things and created a co-dependency of opposites: for example, that life leads to death.

The advances in metallurgic science and the complexity of thought that emerged during the Eastern Zhou Dynasty thus laid the foundation for further technological innovations in swordsmanship. Furthermore, the political situation in the country propagated changes in military strategy and philosophical concepts.[59] Toward the end of the dynasty, warfare began to deviate from the scholarly ideal of the elite fighters. Iron and steel weapons that were stronger and sharper than the older bronze weapons were manufactured in greater quantities and at a lesser expense, and became available also to the general populace. Large citizen armies created wider access to weapons and more consistent methods of training. In the late Warring States period, two-handed steel swords with great cutting capability were becoming more common.

From the Eastern Zhou (770-256 BCE) to Han (202 BCE-220 CE) dynasties, swordsmen would wear their swords slung from a belt, with the "hilt high in front of their body at about stomach level." In the period following the Northern and Southern dynasties (317-589 CE), jian were also worn suspended by two straps from a belt.[60] By contrast, commoners carried the sword on the back if they had long distances to walk and did not predict a need to use the weapon. If conflict were expected, one might decide to prepare the sword by carrying it in the hand. This way one would eliminate the time it took to unsheathe it.[61]

The way in which one transferred a weapon to another person further reinforced the power one afforded the sword. Giving another person a weapon was a gesture of respect: This person was now armed and had the ability to hurt. Or he could choose to use the weapon for the protection of self and others. "A weapon given is [thus] a measure of trust from one to another. [One gives] the weapon as protection, as a practical means of survival and as a means to say that the person gifted is important."[62] Because of these considerations, the sword should be transferred while held vertically with the point up. Or in case of the dao, it should be transferred while held horizontally with the cutting edge facing the swordsman in charge of the transfer. Although transferring the sword with the handle toward the receiving swordsman might seem like a gesture of respect, it also provided him an opportunity to draw the sword and execute an immediate attack against the original owner. Proper etiquette demanded caution, particularly when one did not know where true friendship lay.[63]

Despite the political situation and the changes in military strategy and philosophical concepts in the Zhou Dynasty, the nobility continued to hold most of the ruling power which resulted in fragmentation of the dynasty. In 221 BCE, the emerging state of Qin replaced the Zhou.

THE SWORD IN THE QIN AND HAN DYNASTIES (221 BCE-220 CE)

When the state of Qin annexed the lands of its rivals, a new epoch began for China. As the Qin armies fought for the unification of the empire, long jian made of iron gained popularity. "Some people believe that the success of the Qin in defeating its rivals and in unifying the country is largely due to the use of iron jian."[64] The thousands of weapons uncovered with the Terra Cotta Army of the first emperor of Qin, including swords, spear tips, and arrow heads further demonstrate that the people had considerable knowledge of metallurgic science and had established standards for weapon production.[65] The Terra Cotta weapons reveal scientific knowledge of the production of alloys; for example, how the hardness of material was determined by the proportion of copper to tin. A layer of rustproof chromic salt oxide covering some of these weapons has origins that date to 700 BCE.[66] "This invention was long lost for 2,000 years before modern similar processes were developed . . . in 1937 and the 1950s by Germans and Americans respectively."[67]

The Han Dynasty which followed the short Qin expanded the empire and secured a trade route (the Silk Road) across Central Asia. In the early Han frequent clashes occurred along China's northern border. Campaigns were carried out to protect the empire from the Huns, a Central Asian nomadic people.[68] In these campaigns the Chinese armies used a form of jian that was slender with a "double-edged blade tapering to a point." This sword could be maneuvered with one or two hands depending on its length, and "could be used for either slashing or thrusting."[69] The blade of the jian was divided into three sections of unequal sharpness. The tip was used mainly for thrusting attacks. The part of the blade extending from the tip to the center could achieve great speed in a sideways cut, and was therefore efficient for slashing across soft tissue areas such as the underarm or thigh, or behind the knee joint. These targets were also normally open to attack on an opponent wearing armor. The armor worn at the time consisted of a type of scale lamellar, with overlapping metal plates sewn onto a background of cloth. Although not particularly protective against edged weapons that could penetrate between the metal plates, the armor came with the benefits of decreased weight and increased flexibility.[70]

In downward chopping attacks, the center of the jian could also be used to cleave a skull. The lower part of the blade was normally reserved for blocking or deflecting an opponent's sword; it was thicker and less flexible, and thus benefited a quick deflecting move. By using the portion of the blade that was close to the hand guard in deflecting maneuvers, one prevented the length of the blade from becoming a counterproductive leverage force. Deflections were preferred over blocks because they prevented the "clashing of energy," and allowed one to take advantage of the opponent's motion when counterstriking.[71] While a swordsman wielding the jian used the flat of the sword to block an opponent's attack, a swordsman wielding the dao used the blunt edge for blocking. Because of these design characteristics, the efficient use of the jian required more subtle skills than the dao; however, the jian was still viewed as an attacking weapon which primary purpose in defense was to provide cover for the body, until one could take control of the fight and launch a counterattack.[72]

     Conscript armies comprising infantry and cavalry had now largely replaced the chariots on the battlefield. Cavalry forces would gradually increase in importance, because they alone could keep up with the growing threat of the swift Xiongnu warriors, a nomadic people from Central Asia often identified with the Huns, who controlled a vast steppe empire and complicated the relations with the Han Chinese. Initially the mounted warriors on both sides of the conflict relied heavily on projectile weapons, mainly bow and arrows. As the quality of armor became better for both warrior and horse, the sword proved an effective weapon for defeating enemy combatants. The jian started to lose its value, however, because of "the length of the plane along which it [had] to travel."[73] If a slash were made, the length of the jian required that the sword be fully retracted before a thrust could follow. The weapon therefore proved both clumsy and inefficient when wielded from horseback. As cavalry became more prominent, the curved dao took the place of the straight jian and became the most widely used weapon in China's armies.[74] The long dao proved particularly useful in slashing attacks.[75] Allowing the swordsman to use a single hand in the slashing motion, the dao blade was distinctly suited for cavalry. Additionally, a slash with a curved blade proved the more anatomically correct type of blow for a swordsman performing under the stress of combat, when fine motor skills tended to deteriorate.[76]

The transition from jian to dao was a gradual process, however, that spanned nearly four centuries. By the end of the Eastern Han period (25-220 CE), the dao had effectively replaced the jian as the basic sidearm for cavalrymen. The sturdy, single edged dao sabers of this time were efficient slashing weapons "that could be used by horsemen against either foot soldiers or other cavalry, [and were] superior to the relatively fragile jian with its redundant edge."[77] Short dao also continued to see use in walking infantry.[78] Cavalry is thus only a partial explanation for the existence of dao. The popularity of the dao might stem not from its ease of draw from horseback and superior slashing capabilities, but from the fact that a curved sword is stronger than a straight sword. Enemy tactics and strategy were thus not the only factors that influenced sword design. Principles relating to metallurgic science and physics also played an important role.[79]

The jian, however, transcended time and continued to be carried by the nobility. It was viewed as an extraordinary weapon used for building character and discipline. The use of the jian during the unification of the empire might also have contributed to it becoming a symbol of moral values. A 2,000-year old stone carving depicts Yu Nü, a female jian master performing her skills in front of King Yue, wielding the sword in a high position above her head in what appears to be a circular motion, perhaps with the intent to avoid halting the sword's momentum. Aesthetically pleasing (flowing and circular) moves with the sword swung above the head, however, were impractical for the battlefield. It is thus unlikely that a straight double edged sword would have been handled in a manner where a small miscalculation could have resulted in an inadvertent cut to the swordsman wielding the weapon.[80]

In the Han Dynasty, *wu* (military) yielded to *wen* (civil) under the influence of such thinkers as Confucius and Laozi. *Wu*, it was believed, should be resorted to only when *wen* had been exhausted and no other possibilities remained.[81] However, as Han rule collapsed China came to experience several decades of civil war. "Peasant rebellions and the rise of powerful generals . . . contributed to the fall of the empire." A growing population and increasing wealth resulted in financial difficulties, rivalries, and complex political institutions. Large land-owning families gained even greater prominence. In addition to these internal difficulties, China was repeatedly invaded from the north.[82] The land was divided into the so-called Three Kingdoms of Wei, Wu, and Shu; each claiming Imperial legitimacy.[83]

Relief scene of archers with bows and arrows and infantry with shields and swords, carved on a tomb brick, from the Chinese Han Dynasty. Image source: Gary Lee Todd, reproduced under Wikimedia Commons license.

THE SWORD IN THE THREE KINGDOMS PERIOD (220-263 CE)

When the Han Dynasty stood on the verge of collapse, an influential member of the Daoist Xu clan recommended Zhuge Liang, a military strategist, to the warrior chief. Zhuge Liang, born around the year 180 CE of the Eastern Han Dynasty, assumed positions of responsibility in both civil and military leadership, and came to play a role as strategic advisor in the power struggles that followed the fall of the Han. Zhuge Liang reveals in *The Way of the General* an undercurrent of Daoist thought and its application to swordsmanship.[84]

Swordsmanship skill and accuracy were coupled with clarity of mind. In a letter to his nephew, Zhuge Liang wrote: "Aspirations should remain lofty and far-sighted . . . Detach from emotions and desires." Focus was placed on the promotion of welfare and the elimination of violence. Ideally an acquaintance or relationship should continue "unfading through the four seasons," and become "increasingly stable as it passes through ease and danger." To his son, Zhuge Liang pointed out that "without detachment, there is no way to clarify the will."[85] A Daoist inspired swordsman would approach his opponent without thought of loss or gain, and with the goal to restore harmony. Rather than getting caught up in a power struggle for the prospect of winning, the swordsman would simply think of employing the sword in the opposite direction of his own being.[86] He would use the sword as if it were an extension of his arm, and blend with his opponent's motion until self and opponent became one. This detachment from self also contributed to calmness, or the feeling that one had no opponent.[87] The principle of detachment was further related to the *wen* and the *wu*, the civil and the martial, which balanced virtue with power and were developed as parts of the same entity.[88] According to the ancient Chinese sword master Yuh Niuy, "When the Way is battle, be full-spirited within. But outwardly show calm and be relaxed. Appear to be as gentle as a fair lady, but react like a vicious tiger."[89]

Enlightened swordsmen drew upon both Daoist principles and Confucian ethics in their attempts to further the ideal that once the violence (the threat) had been removed, the sword should be re-sheathed. The model of excellence was to remove the violence by doing as little damage as possible; for example, by cutting off the opponent's thumb so that he could no longer grasp a weapon, but sparing his life. (As late as the eleventh century CE, a Chinese Buddhist suggested that "putting on armor is not the way to promote a country's welfare, it is for eliminating violence."[90]) However, this ideal could be somewhat deceiving. Although the sword was viewed as the "harmonizer," people would frequently lapse into greater violence than the situation called for. The stronger, wealthier, and more powerful ruling class used the sword for the purpose of oppressing the weaker people of society. Such happenings demonstrate that the restoration of harmony through the elimination of violence had the capacity to become counterproductive forces that created tension between social classes and contributed to greater violence.

The *Hua guan suo zhuan* (the story of Hua Guan Suo), a recently rediscovered Chinese novel first printed in 1478, portrays "chivalric epics sung by east Mongolian minstrels." The story depicts Chinese and Mongolian narratives sharing similar motifs for a period of more than four centuries, and can therefore serve as a source of information about the influence of myth on history. The *Hua guan suo zhuan*, based on the events in the novel *San guo yan yi* (Romance of the Three Kingdoms), contains a description of the twenty-four battles that the hero Guan Suo fought. Although these battles depict swordsmanship, the story is not primarily about the martial skills of the swordsman. Rather, the heart of the story is about the hero trying to find his lost father in order that he can establish his legitimacy. This motif is common in Chinese and Mongolian stories because the father was often absent at the birth of the child, due to his participation in warfare and trading.[91]

Another common theme in Chinese story telling is the abandonment and finding of a child, who then grows up to learn martial skills and goes on to fight chivalric battles against other swordsmen. According to the story, Guan Suo was "lost in the turmoil of the lantern festival" and "found by a member of the wealthy Suo family." The family adopted him and sent him to the Daoists for an education in "military tactics, martial arts, morality, and medicine." Guan Suo's skill and courage were tested when he had to uproot a tree in order to defend himself against a band of outlaws "from the mountains surrounding his father's estate." His superhuman strength became a symbol for the "wordliness" of a Daoist swordsman and warrior.

According to legend, Guan Suo engaged in twenty-three additional fights, in which he had to face the common elements of battle: "threat, the raising of troops, the arming of the general, the exchange of insults, boasting, battle, the hero's victory, and feasting." Other qualities included the arming of the hero, the intention to kill, and the rewarding of the helpers after the battle when the losers would plead for mercy and offer to perform menial duties for the hero victor. He would then pardon the enemy and integrate them into his own forces.[92] The story thus demonstrates how harmony was restored by removing the violence and re-sheathing the "sword," and by sparing the enemy his life.

Following the Three Kingdoms period and the collapse of the Jin Dynasty in 317 CE, nearly three centuries of disunity afflicted China. Military authority was delegated to princes of the Imperial family, while barbarian groups focused on defending the frontier. Cavalry gained prominence as the need to stand up to the nomads increased. The important part to note about this period is that it coincides with the appearance of stirrups. This invention would lead to significant changes in the methods of warfare and military organization, particularly with respect to wielding weapons from horseback. The stirrup assisted the warrior in several ways: It allowed him to mount the horse easier when carrying a weapon, it allowed him to pull a strong bow from horseback, and it allowed him to wield a sword in a sweeping motion without fear of losing balance or falling off the horse due to the momentum during the maneuver.[93]

Although cavalry had gained importance as early as the Qin and Han dynasties, its use did not change much until after the fall of the Jin—in the Qin and Han dynasties, emphasis was still placed on infantry foot soldiers over cavalry by a ratio of about three to one, as evidenced by the pottery figures uncovered with the Terra Cotta Army of the first emperor of Qin—when light cavalry experienced more sudden advancements during the continued attempts to deal with the Xiongnu horsemen. This rebellious period fostered new innovations that benefited the mounted warrior. It may also have been "the increasing use of armored cavalry that provided the incentive and favorable environment for the development and widespread use of the stirrup." The armor of the riders in China underwent a number of changes in the centuries following the Three Kingdoms period. For example, double-faced and cord-and-plaque armor were developed, which culminated in the cuirassiers of the Sui and early Tang dynasties. The stirrup allowed one to maintain one's seat easier under the weight of the heavy armor.[94]

Difficulties exist, however, with respect to determining exactly where the stirrup originated, and its cause of invention. The stirrup appeared approximately simultaneously among the Chinese and their enemies along the northern border. Its appearance might thus have been a result of a mounted people who sought to make riding less tiring, or it might have been a result of a people unused to riding who sought to obtain "the skills necessary to meet the needs of cavalry warfare."[95] Either way, new innovations in sword making did not occur until swords began to migrate across Asia in great numbers during the Tang Dynasty (a happening for which the Sui Dynasty receives credit).

THE SWORD IN THE SUI DYNASTY
(581-618 CE)

In the Sui dynasty, metallurgic science had improved to the point that high quality steel blades could be produced. Many of the Chinese swords now traveled to Japan, sometimes directly from China and sometimes via the way of Korea.[96] Since the Japanese had adopted Chinese sword manufacturing techniques from the later Han and continued to do so into the early Tang Dynasty, Chinese sword manufacturing became the foundation of the Japanese sword for nearly half of a millennium.[97]

Two Chinese swords from 600 CE excavated in 1929 at the Imperial Tomb, Pei-Chueu-Shan, in Honan Province, the eastern capital of the Sui and Tang dynasties, show a close relationship to Japanese art. "The first sword is the same in construction and quality as the sword of the Emperor Shomu in the Shosoin at Nara, which is described in the presentation book (756 CE) of the temple of Todaiji as 'one large Chinese sword adorned with gold and silver.'"[98] Since Honan Province was a well-traveled location, it seems natural that craftsmanship would have been exchanged between China and its Central Asiatic neighbors. These swords also bear resemblances to swords found in South Russia, particularly with respect to the carvings on the pommel and the shape of the hand guards. Both of these Chinese swords are of straight shape and similar length, and with nearly identical handles and pommels (one is carved with dragons, the other with a phoenix). The scabbard fittings and ornaments suggest that the swords were slung. This is an interesting observation indicating that the swords were used from horseback (straight swords were typically not wielded from horseback), because the nomads would naturally sling their swords in order to prevent the weapon from interfering with their movements.[99]

As technological science advanced, rather than inventing new swords, the basic ideas of the older swords were preserved and refined. A sword is composed primarily of two parts: the blade which is used for cutting or thrusting, and the hilt which is used for gripping the weapon. Any sword, however, regardless of geographical area, had to have certain qualities in order to be a functional combat arm. First, it had to be properly balanced and of sufficient mass. If it lacked mass, it would also lack the ability to deliver a powerful cut. If it lacked balance, it would be too heavy at the hilt and feel dead in the swordsman's hand, or it would be too heavy at the tip and be difficult to recover after making a cut. Second, the sword had to have an overall weight that proved sufficient for making a decisive blow, yet it had to be light enough to preserve the strength of the swordsman. Some modern accounts attempting to recreate Chinese sword fighting assert that swords weighed up to forty pounds. This claim can be contested. A long weapon such as a sword, because of its moment of inertia, the distribution of mass, and the axis of rotation, would seem heavy when set in motion even at an overall weight of only a few pounds. Moreover, a sword is only useful when in motion. Examinations of artifacts indicate that jian had blades of varied length between 18 inches (for a short sword) and 32 inches (for a long sword), and weighed between one and a half and two pounds. The hilt would add an additional 4 to 9 inches to the overall length. Although a two-pound sword may appear too light to the uninitiated, note that the weight of the jian coincides with the weight of the medieval European longsword, which typically weighed between three and four pounds and measured 36 to 48 inches in length.[100] By contrast, a forty-pound sword would require extraordinary strength to wield, and would be nearly useless for any kind of combat extending beyond a first strike.

Swords were sometimes buried with their owner, which seems to imply that they were custom made and highly valued pieces of weaponry and craftsmanship. Conflicting research indicates that this was not necessarily the case. Most Chinese jian and dao have small variations in length, no more than a few inches, which suggests that the swords were not custom made to fit the build of the swordsman. In addition, the variations in decoration of the hilts and blades seem to be limited.[101] Although sword artifacts display signs of craftsmanship and value, most swords were likely part of the common interchange of weaponry between China and other neighboring Asian countries, rather than manufactured to specific lengths or styles.[102] Moreover, although jian were used in the strife for refinement and perfection of character, swords were primarily instruments of combat. They had hard and sharp edges which enabled the weapon to penetrate the target—including clothing, armor, flesh, and even bone if one wished to dismember the enemy—with speed and ease. Swords also had to be flexible in order to withstand the stress associated with cutting, deflecting, and blocking maneuvers. A well-crafted sword could hold an edge, and enabled the swordsman to execute several cuts before re-sharpening the blade.[103]

Jian were expensive to manufacture, and the poorer people who constituted the bulk of Chinese society (about 90 percent were farmers or artisans) could not afford to own jian. The market for jian swordsmiths thus focused on the aristocrats who needed swords to protect themselves and their estates, and higher ranking military men who carried swords as part of their official regalia. The aristocrats and the military is "estimated to have made up no more than 2 or 3 percent of the total population" in Imperial China. The Chinese people were also influenced by social restrictions, which dictated who should be allowed to wear swords in each social class, and when. People were expected to maintain the social order by understanding "their place" and conforming to set rules.[104] While jian continued to be carried by the nobility, most dao sabers, by contrast, were constructed for military use rather than individual practice; they were mass produced and made to regulation specification.[105]

espite the Sui's short four-decade lifespan, it managed to unite China and end centuries of division between rival regimes. Internal administration improved. The administrative structure of the period is reflected in the social restrictions placed on the populace, in the mass production of weapons, and in the small variations in sword length and decorative motifs as a result of the requirement to wear "regulation" swords. Confucianism regained some of its popularity with the growing importance of the nobility. The spread of Buddhism was also highly encouraged. However, the desire to expand the borders resulted in several military campaigns toward the south and north. Defeats in Korea led to further attacks on China by the Eastern Turks and a subsequent split of Chinese society.[106] Although the disunity of the preceding centuries had resulted in declining relationships with neighboring countries and China again stood on the verge of collapse, perhaps the greatest accomplishment of the Sui was that it managed to reestablish trade relations and promote the exchange of ideas, goods, and weapons, as evidenced by Chinese sword artifacts of this period bearing resemblances to swords found in Japan and South Russia.

THE SWORD IN THE TANG AND SONG DYNASTIES (618-1279 CE)

The greatest advances in metallurgic science came during the Tang (618-907 CE) and Song (960-1279) dynasties. China's steel production allowed the country to become a powerful military force in Asia.[107] The exact composition of the steel used in swords was an art form. The laws of physics and the limitations of science and invention dictated a sword's combat qualities. Swordsmiths focused on crafting hard and double edged blades that were resilient but could withstand the forces of combat. A sword that was too hard would be brittle and break upon contact with the target. By contrast, a sword that was too soft would be unable to hold a sharp edge and would thus be useless in combat, particularly against armored enemy troops. Normally, high-carbon steel formed the edge. This hard outer layer which enveloped a softer core was folded upon itself for greater strength, allowing the blade to be sharpened several times without risk of grinding it down to the core.

Many of the Chinese swords were constructed in lamellar design, utilizing hundreds of alternating layers of harder and softer steel. The layered construction, known as *qiangang* (inserted steel), commonly used in the single edged dao was a widely used form of forging a strong blade. The high-carbon steel edge was sandwiched between softer material made of alternating layers of iron and steel. When the blade had been polished by a skilled swordsmith, it achieved structural strength as well as a surface pattern, known as Damascus, which added considerable beauty to the blade.[108] The double edged jian (in addition to some dao) commonly relied on the *sanmei* three-plate construction. Finally, there was *twistcore*, which involved the twisting of two parallel bars of hard and soft steel. These were welded and hammered out into a single blade. Swordsmiths from all parts of the world have relied on a process of heating and cooling in liquid in order to achieve a hard blade. But the Chinese developed the method further by learning how to treat only the edge with heat, rather than the entire blade. This process added to the overall strength of the sword.[109]

Although the curved blade of the dao appears to have existed in some form throughout most of the history of edged weaponry, "it rose to prominence during the conquest of the Turkic and Mongol tribes." Knowledge of sword making traveled from China to Japan. Japanese samurai blades were originally straight and owe their curved shape in part to the attempted Mongol invasion of Japan in the thirteenth century CE, when the Japanese "discovered their straight blades were ineffective against the Mongol armor." Other evidence suggests that swords evolved into many varieties due to the influence of war and commerce. For example, the straight jian was exported to Japan during the Tang Dynasty, and evolved into the curved shape of the Japanese *katana*. Chinese and Korean swordsmiths also migrated to Japan to transmit their skill at forge-welding, folding, and differential heat treatment. Furthermore, trade along the Silk Road spread knowledge of sword making in several directions. For example, Indian and Islamic swords display Chinese decorative motifs.

Likewise, "Islamic-inspired faceted blades and fullering appeared on dao blades."[110]

Knowledge of sword manufacturing traveled full circle in the Asian world. Japan learned from China and Korea how to construct high quality swords; however, China came to appreciate the craftsmanship behind the Japanese sabers in the Song Dynasty. The exchange and export of swords between Japan and China is evident in some of the ancient Chinese poetry. Around 1060 CE, the renowned Chinese statesman and poet Ouyang Xiu wrote: "From the land of the rising sun come precious swords . . . / With scabbards of fragrant wood, sharkskin-covered, and bearing / Designs in silver and gold, trappings of brass and bronze." Although this verse speaks of the high value one placed on the sword, some swords captured as booty from coastal pirates varied in quality.[111] Top quality luxurious Japanese blades, however, were imported to China as collector's items.[112]

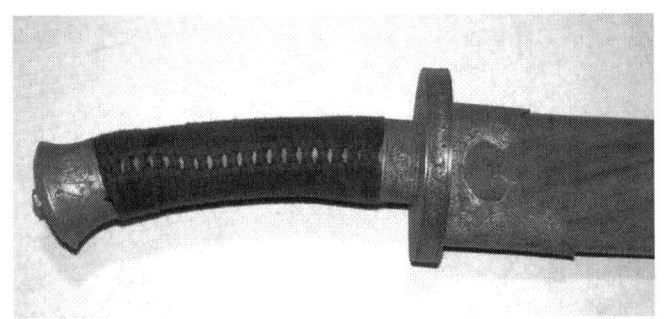

Ornamental handle of a Chinese dao. Image source: Lawrence Kane.

Li Ch'üan, a political official who flourished in the mid-eighth century CE, contributed to military thought in this period. When he managed to offend the reigning prime minister, Li Lin-fu, he was demoted in rank and became a Daoist recluse. He is known to have written five works, one of which is *The Secret Classic of T'ai-po*. According to this treatise, military prowess comes when one has investigated the enemy thoroughly. First then can plans be laid and warfare executed with ease and without worries of success or failure. To accomplish a successful investigation of the enemy, one must become "a part of other men." One must have the "intuitive powers to recognize objective circumstances and enemy intentions and to act upon that awareness." Li Ch'üan believed that war was a "self-conscious thrust for personal or national aggrandizement, resulting not in homeostasis but in chaos and renewed conflict, due to human insensitivity." He stressed that weapons in order to be awe-inspiring should only be used on timely occasions and otherwise stored away. Weapons that were displayed too often or were overused would lose their respect and power. A principal emphasis on *wu*, the martial, would therefore be only sparingly effectual.[113]

    The military organization lost some of its prestige in the Song, in part because of the resistance to displaying the sword on other than special occasions, and in part because the "weakening of the military coincided with the rise of strong nomadic nations on China's borders."[114] Despite the widespread migration of swords across geographical regions and cultures, difficulty existed with the transfer of knowledge to future generations Chinese. While sword technology reached great heights in

China, it suffered in continuity. Methods of sword making were considered military secrets and failed to be passed along to coming generations who, therefore, had to work on decoding "cryptic poems and songs" in order to rediscover old techniques.[115] In the late eleventh century CE, the Chinese developed the *zhanmadao*, an anti-cavalry weapon, in response to the need for Song infantry troops to cut through heavily armored cavalry riders and horses, mainly Tibetans, Mongols, and Khitans, an ethnic group that dominated much of Manchuria. As recorded in the *Official History of the Song Dynasty* for the year 1072 CE:

> In the fifth year of the Xining, the Emperor (Shenzong) showed the zhanmadao to the Court Official Cai Ting, who commented on its excellent workmanship and its ease of use. He thereby ordered the sword to be mass-produced in tens of thousands by the Imperial smiths to be presented to his subordinates and men.[116]

The zhanmadao, which was nearly three and a half feet in length, had a single edged broad blade and a handle long enough to accommodate two hands. The strength and quality of this sword was verified through a procedure where twenty to thirty of every batch of one hundred swords were chosen randomly and tested by cutting through plate armor or copper coins. When the soldiers who had been formed into a special vanguard unit confronted the enemy cavalry, they bent low and chopped with the sword at the legs of the horses bearing the enemy. This weapon saw continued use by soldiers in the Ming Dynasty guarding the northern border against Mongol cavalry. "During the Qing, it was also the standard equipment of the Green Standard Army, which [was] composed mainly of ethnic Chinese soldiers."[117] One can thus discern a relationship between the length and strength of the sword reflected in the need to wield it with two hands, and the military conditions of the period which necessitated fighting heavily armored cavalry.

THE SWORD IN THE MING AND QING DYNASTIES (1368-1912 CE)

The Ming Dynasty (1368-1644 CE) was a period of restoration and reorganization. The practices of Confucianism were restored. Sword design and versatility experienced a considerable degree of experimentation. The nomadic tribes of Central Asia used saber-type swords with a curved cutting edge. Chinese encounters between these nomadic tribes and the geographical regions of Asia, Eastern Europe, and the Middle East led to the development of the *peidao*.[118] This type of saber was "designed to be wielded primarily in one hand and to be worn on the left side in a scabbard slung by straps or cords from a waist belt."[119] The swordsman would draw the weapon with the edge up in a cross-draw with the right hand.[120] This type of draw allowed him to execute a cutting stroke within the movement of the draw. Although the Chinese nobility continued to favor the straight jian, the peidao was popular with the aristocracy in the early Ming Dynasty. Several interesting relationships also existed between swords of different periods and geographical regions, particularly with respect to the design of the hilt. For example, some hilts on jian swords, "depicted on Ming Dynasty imperial tomb guardian figures," were styled after the peidao.[121]

The saber thus came to exist alongside the straight sword for several hundred years. Cavalrymen and foot soldiers alike carried the saber, as did anyone who favored slashing over thrusting capabilities on the field of battle. Shape varied, but the blades were normally long and heavy and had only a slight taper along the entire blade. Some blades extended straight from the hilt until reaching the sharpened part of the back edge (in the West, the unsharpened part is called the *forte* and normally extends a few inches forward of the hilt), where it assumed a slight and gradual upward arc until reaching the tip. Others had a sharper acceleration of the curve from the end of the forte to the tip. Still others, particularly the *piandao* designed for efficient slashing following a draw-cut at close range, portrayed a sharper curvature. Saber-type swords proved well suited for "powerful sweeping cuts from horseback."[122] The rider would sweep his arm in a circular motion and slash through the target. Sabers were also used by the Turkic peoples, and would spread to regions of Persia, India, and Eastern Europe as a consequence of Mongol-initiated wars.[123] Several practical design characteristics such as a downward curving grip, blade shape, fuller design, and the presence of a back edge indicate a strong influence of Chinese sabers on the Islamic world, and vice versa. Aesthetic design characteristics were shared and transmitted between the geographical regions. For example, Chinese dragon and phoenix motifs have been found on Persian swords, and Islamic segmented fullers and chiseled animal motifs have been found on Chinese swords.[124]

China also imported sabers from Japan, which resulted in that some parts of the sword changed to reflect this foreign influence. These changes were particularly noticeable with respect to the hand guard, which, in Japan, had assumed a disk shape (unlike the cruciform shape, technically called a "cross-guard," commonly used in China).[125] This small guard was thought to provide greater protection to the swordsman's hand against the cuts of an enemy's weapon. The grip was large enough to accommodate about a hand and a half, or one full hand and two or three fingers of the second hand. The sword in this period was therefore primarily a one-handed weapon. By contrast, the Japanese katana had a longer grip, which served as an extension of the tang for the purpose of moving the point of percussion to its proper place in the one-third of the blade nearest the tip. (A pommel on the Chinese swords helped adjust the point of percussion and balance the blade.[126]) The Japanese swords could therefore accommodate two hands easier, and became much sought-after commodities considered luxury items. More than 75,000 Japanese swords were exported to China.[127]

Although full two-handed swords existed in China, they were not as common as the one-handed version. The sword was normally wielded with one hand, but could be held with two hands if one needed power for a heavy chopping or thrusting technique. If he sustained an injury to the sword hand, proficiency with the other hand might allow the swordsman to switch hands and continue the fight.[128] As previously noted, during the period of cultural exchange in the Tang Dynasty a certain type of long saber was used mainly as an anti-cavalry weapon, and may have been adopted as a result of exposure to the swords of the Japanese pirates along China's southeastern coast. This long two-handed sword vanished from Chinese history after the fall of the Tang Dynasty when Chinese society became less martial. Low wages paid to swordsmiths and poor administration by the Imperial authorities in northern China might also have contributed to a decline in sword making skills.[129] The long saber reappeared during the Ming Dynasty, when General Qi Jiguang had his troops use it against enemies on the Mongol border around 1560 CE. "Commanding up to 100,000 troops on the Mongol border, General Qi found this [sword] so effective that up to 40 percent of his commandos had it as a weapon."[130]

Qi Jiguang is recognized as one of the most successful generals of the Ming Dynasty. Noted for his severe discipline and intense training, he led an army comprising uniformed regulars and civilian auxiliaries against Japanese pirates in Zejiang province.[131] He stipulated that the cutting edge of the sword should be made of the best steel, free of impurities, and that all excess metal was to be filed away where the back of the blade joined the edge.[132] It might also be interesting to note that, although the curved saber was developed mainly as a weapon to be wielded from horseback, the long two-handed saber was developed particularly as an anti-cavalry weapon to be wielded by foot soldiers. Its length, which necessitated two-handed use, would have made it a highly impractical weapon when wielded from horseback.

The *yanmaodao*, another type of Chinese saber used in China from the Ming (1368-1644 CE) and through the first half of the Qing Dynasty (1644-1912 CE), relied on the combined features of the straight and curved blade. The arc of the cutting edge toward the point gave the swordsman the ability to deliver devastating cuts. At the same time, the thickness of the spine gave this saber enough strength to surpass the double edged jian in cutting power. The lack of a curve for most of the blade, and the sharp tip, also gave the swordsman the ability to execute straight thrusts. A drawback was that these sorts of "combined-feature blades" normally achieved only mid-range versatility; they were highly efficient neither for slashing nor thrusting attacks. The greater curve of the willow-leaf saber, which was widely used in the Ming Dynasty and which became "a sidearm of choice for military men," proved a better slashing weapon, but changed "the balance sufficiently to make it less accurate for the thrust." As a result of new innovations in saber design, powerful cuts could be delivered either from foot or horse. The oxtail saber, which appeared in the late eighteenth century CE and was used mainly by civilians in numerous rebellions fought by peasants, who lacked military training, had a wide blade with increasing width toward the tip, then tapering to a point. This heavy weapon could produce damaging cuts even if the swordsman were untrained.[133] The *dadao*, or fighting sword, the traditional weapon of China's peasant armies, was used in battle as late as the 1930s in the Second Sino-Japanese War.[134]

The sharpening of a sword, from a Ming Dynasty scroll located at the Palace Museum. Image source: Huang Ji, reproduced under Wikimedia Commons license.

Fullers took several shapes. The fuller, sometimes incorrectly called a "blood groove" (some fullers were decorated with a red lacquer), decreased the weight of the blade and added to its strength: "By channeling either side of a thin or 'whippy' blade it becomes stiffer, because any force applied to bend such a blade sideways meets with the greatest amount of resistance that form can supply."[135] A narrow groove was preferable to a broader groove of the same length. Some blades portrayed double fullers and were made of a three-fold structure that included a high carbon layer sandwiched between two softer and more resilient layers of metal.[136] Others, particularly the later slashing-type sabers, portrayed segmented fullers likely inspired by Indian and Persian swords. The blade was welded in different ways. As previously noted, a popular style was the Damascus blade, or flower-patterned steel, which employed several rows of twisted cores of iron and steel laminate. These blades, too, may have been influenced by the well-developed metallurgic traditions of Iran, India, and Central Asia. Many of these weapons may have made their way to China as "trade goods, booty, or travel mementos."[137] The pattern-welded sword was later adopted by Japanese swordsmiths as well.

In the Qing Dynasty, Chinese sword making was further refined and reached new heights. Swordsmiths adhered to standards of craftsmanship and used high quality raw materials for the construction of "regulation" swords, typically 26 inches in length. Military personnel and the Qing aristocracy relied on a style of swordsmanship, known as the older battlefield tradition, which focused on linear moves and cuts designed for quick execution inside of the range of an opponent's weapon.[138] Attendants following the aristocracy bore large and ornate jian swords with blue-green silk wrappings around the handle.[139] The regulation swords carried by military personnel, and the ornate jian carried by attendants to the nobility indicate that China was still very much a bureaucratic society focused on upholding the social order by assigning people and weapons their "proper" places.

In late Imperial China, "the state relied primarily on professional standing armies based on hereditary staffing, with additional conscription from the populace in times of emergency . . . the military was multiethnic (Manchus, Chinese, Mongols). In all these units, soldiers expected their sons to follow them into the ranks. Weapons, dress, and gear were standardized."[140] The armor consisted of large-scale armor made of overlapping plates. Although efficient as protection against a downward cut, it proved less durable against an upward cut that might slide between the plates. Imperial troops also wore lamellar laced with leather for protection. However, both types of armor had openings under the arms for ease of mobility, so the armpits remained susceptible to sword thrusts.[141]

The nineteenth century was marked by internal rebellions. Following China's Taiping Rebellion (1850-1864 CE), one of the most destructive conflicts in Chinese history led by a group of peasant rebels, militia units came to replace the regular army. The training and equipment of these forces differed vastly across regions. While highly modern, well-trained and equipped divisions existed, for example, in the Yangzi region, other areas had to resort to a mass of lower paid and undisciplined provincial soldiers. These armies carried a variety of weapons including swords, spears, and modern rifles and guns.[142] This example from history reinforces the idea that a reason why the sword in China has received relatively little attention in written sources is because the sword, although carried alongside of other weapons, was never the distinct weapon of choice. Rather, it was a practical alternative available, with few exceptions, also to the commoners.

Sword drills from an illustration from the *Wubei Zhi*, a work on military tactics from the early seventeenth century and perhaps the most comprehensive military book in Chinese history. Image source: Mao Yuanyi, reproduced under Wikimedia Commons license.

The Chinese carried the sword well into the twentieth century. Evidence of the sword as a complementary rather than primary weapon can be found as late as 1937 during the War of Resistance, when the Chinese relied on the broadsword (or the dadao fighting sword) against Japanese aggression. "Its single- or two-handed versatility, combined with the tremendous slashing power of its weight-forward blade made [the dadao] the ideal close-quarters weapon."[143] As Japan started its invasion of China, according to General Qin Dechun, the Japanese soldiers "kowtowed before Chinese broadsword holders to beg for mercy." On July 8, 1937 the Japanese used invading infantry and tanks to invade Wanping Town near the Marco Polo Bridge in Northeast China. When the Japanese forces had partially overrun the bridge, the KMT (Kuomintang) forces of about a thousand soldiers received reinforcements that allowed them to retake the bridge, while beheading a considerable number of the Japanese enemy with the broadsword.[144] It can thus be concluded that the Chinese sword, while taking many shapes and seeing a variety of uses throughout its three thousand year long evolutionary process, proved a versatile weapon that managed to survive as a combat arm into near modern day.

CONCLUDING REMARKS

China has enjoyed a long history of sword making. For thousands of years, "soldiers wielding bronze, iron and cold steel defended the realms or marched to glorious conquest."[145] The first bronze swords were created approximately three thousand years ago. In early Chinese history, "when North China was divided among a large number of competing city-states ruled by a warrior aristocracy . . . wars were fought for prestige and honor, more often than for territory."[146] The swords of the Spring and Autumn period were designed for thrusting, not for slashing attacks. The Warring States period saw a number of changes that would alter Chinese warfare. The rise of large armies and the introduction of cavalry resulted in a need for different types of weapons. Close range combat swords complemented halberds "and other chariot-oriented war implements."[147] In the Han Dynasty, iron and steel gradually came to replace the bronze swords. The Chinese perfected their steel processing techniques as early as 300 BCE. Some of the finer developments did not occur in the western world until the nineteenth and twentieth century CE.

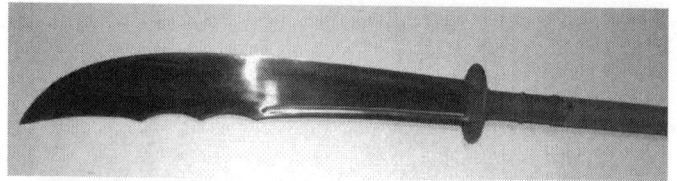

Chinese halberd. Close range combat swords complemented halberds and other chariot-oriented war implements. Image source: Lawrence Kane.

The Chinese were creative with sword designs. The long and unbroken history of the straight-edged jian is a testament to its value as a weapon and symbol of status. China also developed a great variety of sabers; some broad-bladed, others slender and with more gentle curves. Toward the end of the Han Dynasty, as cavalry began to dominate the battlefield, the sword evolved into single edged sabers that were well-suited for mounted warriors. Chinese sword making techniques then spread throughout Asia. Sophisticated methods of forging and heat-treating "predated and indeed were the knowledge base from which the forging of Japanese swords was born. Beautiful and functional laminating and folding patterns, efficient shapes, superior durability and cutting ability were all manifested in ancient Chinese swords."[148] Many of these swords surpassed the performances of the Japanese swords.[149]

The value of Chinese swords is expressed in a poem by Japanese empress Suiko (554-628 CE). When asked about her *Soga*, an aristocratic clan of Korean descent that was influential in the Japanese Imperial Court, she wrote: "Were they swords, they would be the good blades of Kure." (Kure was the

Japanese pronunciation for Wu, one of the three states of China during the Three Kingdoms era. During this period, Japan recruited Chinese swordsmiths.[150] The Chinese sword making techniques of forging, folding, and differential heat treatment came to influence sword production also in other countries in the Far East, including Vietnam and Korea.

The mention of swords in early Chinese poetry and novels is further testament to the unique place the sword holds in Chinese history. Chivalry combat with the sword is portrayed in the historical Chinese novel, *Three Kingdoms*, written by Luó Guànzhōng in the fourteenth century CE.[151] The novel provides insight into how the chivalric heroes of China's past were viewed. The value one placed on swords is evident also in the monument dedicated to Yue Fei, a general who distinguished himself in battle and fought against the invasion of the State of Jin in the Song Dynasty. A statue of General Yue Fei, armed with a sword on the left side of his body, can be viewed at the memorial temple next to the mausoleum of Yue Fei, located at the southern foot of Qixia Hill in Nanjing.[152]

Confucius said, "Without determination, man is an untempered sword."[153] The scholars and literati placed great emphasis on refinement and elegance, and thus trained with the straight double edged jian. Although the sword symbolized Chinese culture, values, and warrior spirit, the rise and fall of China's dynasties along with the internal problems experienced in a class structured society most certainly contributed to fluctuations between the *wen* and the *wu* (the civil and the martial). The propagation of anti-militarist Confucian concepts, however, and the suggestion that the use of force was an indication of failed virtues did not necessarily interfere with winning military victories. Rather, the idea was to use force with foresight and timing. Although the sword would act as the "harmonizer" in order to balance the forces of the universe, the Chinese concept of *ch'i*, or fighting spirit, was defined by Sunzi as the will and intention to enter battle. Ch'i was attained by following three simple steps: Define the objective, assess the situation, and prepare properly. This sequence of organizing military campaigns translated into clarity of vision coupled with skill and accuracy, which further led to the confidence and fighting spirit one needed to proceed into battle.[154] The yin and the yang, the embrace of opposites, were further reflected in the military side of Chinese swordsmanship on the one hand, which evolved from chivalric ideals to the quick killing of the enemy in infantry mass armies and cavalry warfare, and in the civil side of Chinese swordsmanship on the other, which stipulated that sword practice benefited the general populace in their strife for health and perfection of character.

    The Chinese sword has earned a place in the history of edged weaponry, as evidenced by the complex patterns of military and philosophical currents that shaped the sword and its uses. This book has demonstrated that the roots of the Chinese sword are deep. While the sword saw use in battle, ranging from single combat to mass infantry and cavalry warfare from the Zhou Dynasty into near present day, it also found continued value as an instrument of personal growth in martial arts practice. The jian (in particular), but also the dao, "capture the spirit and the craft of an age when men of steel stood toe to toe in mortal combat,"[155] and remain popular weapons of choice in contemporary martial arts schools in Asia and the Western world.

"Now gallants tap their two-edged swords,
And pride and passion swell amain;
Like red stars flashing through the night."[156]

—Du Fu (712-770 CE), one of China's most prominent poets.

NOTES

[1] See David A. Graff and Robin Higham, *A Military History of China* (Boulder, CO: Westview Press, 2002), ix. A full chronology is also readily available from a vast number of Internet resources.

[2] Philip Tom, *The Art of the Chinese Sword*, Fighting Arts, http://www.fightingarts.com/reading/article.php?id=1 28. Philip Tom has more than twenty-five years of experience in the restoration of ancient Chinese swords. Tom provides detailed descriptions of the impressive advancements made in Chinese metallurgic science, particularly during the Tang (618-907 CE) and Song (960-1279 CE) dynasties. He has contributed to the historiography of the field through extensive research of artifacts located at museums in China, France, and Russia, and has made his knowledge public through articles written for the *Metropolitan Museum Journal*. His research ranges from advancements in metallurgic science in early Chinese history to the making of sabers in the Qing Dynasty (1644-1912 CE). See Philip Tom, "Some Notable Sabers of the Qing Dynasty at the Metropolitan Museum of Art," *Metropolitan Museum Journal,* Vol. 36 (2001). Tom describes the great variety of sabers and the migration of sword designs across Asian and Islamic cultures. With few exceptions, however, his treatments are quite technical and do not offer much insight into the philosophical aspects that affected the use of the jian and dao. The Kangxi emperor ruled over all of China from 1661 to 1722 CE. Although he was the longest

reigning emperor of China, he ascended the throne at age seven and, therefore, was subjected to control by his guardians. The Chinese people considered the Kangxi emperor practical and conscientious. Despite having vetoed a request to disarm the people of Shandong Province, he managed to maintain the peace for most of his reign. See Emperor Kangxi History, *Emperor of China – Qing Dynasty*, http://www.paulnoll.com/China/Money/I-money-choices-pic1.html.

[3] See Zhang Yun, *The Art of Chinese Swordsmanship* (Boston, MA: Weatherhill, 1998), 38-39. The jian, due to its straight shape, has two identical edges. The edge at the thumb side of the hand is referred to as the upper edge regardless of the direction it faces at any particular moment. The opposite edge is called the lower edge.

[4] Note the importance of the sword to the cavalryman in China and India. The "sword *(asi)* and the horse *(aswa)* have given the name to the continent of Asia." See E. Jaiwant Paul, *Arms and Armour: Traditional Weapons of India* (Singapore: Lustre Press, 2004), 9.

[5] See Tom, *The Art of the Chinese Sword*. China's Bronze Age began around 2100 BCE. Although many bladed Chinese weapons were considered dao as long as they could cut and slice, this book is concerned primarily with the straight jian sword and the curved dao saber.

[6] See Laurent Murawiec, "China's Grand Strategy is to Make War While Avoiding a Battle," *Armed Forces Journal* (Jul. 2007), http://www.armedforcesjournal.com/2005/11/1164221.

[7]See Alexander Chin, review of *Chinese Swordsmanship: The Yang Family Taiji Jian Tradition*, by Scott Rodell, Sword Forum International, http://swordforum.com/articles/css/chineseswordsmanship.php. Scott M. Rodell, a student of Chinese history and collector of Chinese arms, has contributed to the field with information about the history and practical uses of the jian through his book, *Chinese Swordsmanship: The Yang Family Taiji Jian Tradition*. Rodell describes the sword techniques from a logical perspective, relying on the principles of physics. Rodell's book is somewhat limited as a source for historical combat, however, due to its greater treatment of the practice of swordsmanship for aesthetic reasons and health purposes. Early firearms failed to help cavalry, because these weapons were inaccurate and thus ineffective when used from horseback. See Kenneth Chase, *Firearms: A Global History to 1700* (New York, NY: Cambridge University Press, 2003), 23. Confucianism stresses "the importance of routine practice of rituals, and believes [that] external rituals [such as sword practice] cultivate inner virtues." From Miles Maochun Yu, conversation with the author, Norwich University, VT, 2007.

[8]Tom, *The Art of the Chinese Sword*.

[9]See Mark Beale, *Terra Cotta Weapons: Weapons of Ancient China*, http://dana.ucc.nau.edu/msb46/Weapons_of_Ancient_China.html. Mark Beale has conducted research and analysis of the weapons of ancient China. In addition to his treatise on metallurgic science, he examines the physics of slicing versus stabbing attacks. The

strength of Beale's studies lies in his examination of what is commonly called the "Eighteen Weapons" (a phrase that refers to the arms used by China's ancient warriors), divided into nine long and nine short weapons including knives, swords, spears, axes, pikes, and halberds. A weakness of this particular source is the shallow treatment he gives each weapon. The information he provides therefore fails to contribute sufficiently to discerning relationships between the jian and the dao. See also Wu Dingbo and Patrick D. Murphy, *Handbook of Chinese Popular Culture* (Westport, CT: Greenwood Publishing Group, 1994), 162.

[10] See Graff and Higham, 25.

[11] See Ralph Sawyer and Mei-Chün Sawyer, *The Seven Military Classics of Ancient China* including the *Art of War* (Boulder, CO: Westview Press, 1993).

[12] See Graff and Higham, 40.

[13] The uses and developments of Japanese swords have been followed with interest internationally. Miyamoto Musashi's *Book of Five Rings*, although written from the perspective of one particular samurai, is a practical and insightful guide to swordsmanship and might be the most widely studied Japanese treatise on the subject of the sword. See Miyamoto Musashi, *Book of Five Rings*, translated by Thomas Cleary (Boston, MA: Shambhala, 2005). Although the Japanese developed sword making into an art form, they relied on immigrant swordsmiths from China and Korea. See Tom, *The Art of the Chinese Sword*.

[14] In order to conduct a meaningful study of the sword, one might start by breaking China's

history into separate periods and examine the changes that occurred in the civil and military order. Each period can then be viewed by its specific characteristics. For example, in the Spring and Autumn period (722-481 BCE), "warfare was mainly the province of the aristocratic elites." During the Warring States period (453-221 BCE) and Han (202 BCE-220 CE), large armies were built by relying on conscript peasants. "Later periods saw the hereditary military households of 'militias' of farmer soldiers." See Graff and Higham, 10.

[15] Adrian Ko, *The Development of Swords Through the Ages*, http://www.arscives.com/gallery/en/fireandforge/development.htm. Adrian Ko's approach to the history of swordsmanship in China offers a unique perspective, particularly with respect to the cross-cultural exchange of swords in Asia.

[16] See Bai Yunxiang, "Origin of Bronze and Iron in China," *Institute of Archaeology* (Beijing, China: Chinese Academy of Social Sciences, 2005).

[17] William Watson, review of *Chinese Bronze Age Weapons: The Werner Jannings Collection in the Chinese National Palace Museum*, by Max Loehr, *The Burlington Magazine,* Vol. 99, No. 654 (Sep. 1957), 316.

[18] See S. Howard Hansford, review of "Chinese Bronze Age Weapons: The Werner Jannings Collection in the Chinese National Palace Museum," by Max Loehr, *Bulletin of the School of Oriental and African Studies, University of London*, Vol. 19, No. 3 (1957), 605-606. Professor Max Loehr, an authority on Chinese weapons, has conducted significant studies of the Werner Jannings Collection

of Chinese bronze weapons, located in the Chinese National Palace Museum.

[19]Few original texts exist about metallurgy and the development of iron and steel used in the construction of Chinese swords. There seems to be more philosophical tradition than actual military treatises surrounding swordsmanship. Much of the research that historians have done on the subject is therefore related to direct examination of artifacts and arms collections housed at various museums.

[20]See Christopher C. Rand, "Li Ch'üan and Chinese Military Thought," *Harvard Journal of Asian Studies*, Vol. 39, No. 1 (Jun. 1979), 107-109. Christopher Rand discusses the relationship between martiality and civility, and demonstrates how this relationship must be "proper" in order for the state to achieve its goals.

[21]The Zhou Dynasty was the longest lasting of the Chinese dynasties, and gave China many of the political and cultural traits that came to dominate later periods. Note that the Eastern Zhou Dynasty was divided into the Spring and Autumn (722-481 BCE) and Warring States (453-221 BCE) periods, so named after historical chronicles of the time.

[22]See Scott M. Rodell, *Chinese Swordsmanship: The Yang Family Taiji Jian Tradition* (Annandale, VA: Seven Stars Books and Video, 2005), xi.

[23]See Graff and Higham, 20. "The Mandate of Heaven was a political-social philosophy that served as the basic Chinese explanation for the success and failure of monarchs and states down to the end of the empire in 1912 CE. Whenever a dynasty fell, the reason invariably offered by China's sages was that it

had lost the moral right to rule, which is given by Heaven alone. In this context, Heaven did not mean a personal god but a cosmic all-pervading power." See Chinese Cultural Studies, *The Mandate of Heaven: Selections from the Shu Jing*, http://acc6.its.brooklyn.cuny.edu/~phalsall/texts/shu-jing.html.

[24] See Graff and Higham, 20.

[25] See Rand, 110.

[26] See Zhang Yun, 15-17. Archaeological discoveries have revealed that jian were initially particular to the northwestern part of China, until the weapon spread also to central and southern China.

[27] See Watson, 316. Max Loehr observes that certain types of swords in the Werner Jannings Collection located in the Chinese National Palace Museum appear to be of foreign origin. He attributes the foreign characteristics of these weapons to the contact that occurred between the nomad herdsmen of the Eurasian steppes and western Asia. Many of the Chinese swords also traveled to Japan, sometimes directly from China and sometimes via the way of Korea.

[28] See Bai Yunxiang.

[29] See Chinese Swords, *Chronology Table on 2500 Years of Chinese Sword Technical Developments*, http://chineseswords.freewebspace.com/about.html.

[30] See Rodell, 15-19.

[31] See Zhuangzi, translated by Herbert A. Giles, first published in 1889, Galileo Library, http://www.galileolibrary.com/ebooks/as07/chuangtzu_page_24.htm.

³²Jim Hwang, "A Swordsmith and His Legacy," *Taiwan Review* (Nov. 2001), http://taiwanreview.nat.gov.tw/site/Tr/ct.asp?xItem=672&CtNode=128.

³³See Zhang Yun, 77-79. According to Zhang Yun, in the Han dynasties (202 BCE-220 CE) and the Western Jin Dynasty (265-317 CE), books about jian principles became more widespread. An example is the *Jian Dao* (Way of the Jian or Thirty-Eight Topics), which, unfortunately, does not appear to exist in English translation. In addition to examining the practice and skill of the swordsman, Zhang Yun touches on metallurgic science with focus on the changing shape of the jian: from short, broad, and thick to long, narrow, and thin as reflected, for example, in some of the swords of the Tang Dynasty (618-907 CE).

³⁴See Thomas Chen, *Swordsmiths Ganjiang and Oyue*, http://thomaschen.freewebspace.com/custom2.html.

³⁵Hwang.

³⁶Zhang Yun, 265.

³⁷Ibid., 21-23.

³⁸The jian was sharp at the tip and along the upper part of the edges on both sides, and could therefore be used in very subtle movements that did not require a great deal of strength. Because of these characteristics, it was said that the mind, rather than the body, guided the sword. See Zhang Yun, 261.

³⁹Ibid., 44. This idea can be substantiated by noting that fine motor skills such as manipulating a pencil require the use of the thumb and index finger, while gross motor skills such as gripping a pull-up

bar require the use of the part of the hand toward the little finger.

[40] Rodell, 36, 62 & 259. The jian was viewed as the "general of all weapons." The fighting skills of King Yue and King Wu, who fought each other in 494 BCE, "and the high quality of their jian have been praised in many legends. The accuracy of these stories, however, was not appreciated until the graves of the two kings were discovered and their actual weapons unearthed." See Zhang Yun, 15-17.

[41] See Rand, 107-109.

[42] During the time of chivalry, tricking an opponent was equivalent to cheating. The bigger armies and better equipment of the Warring States period, however, led to that victory became the primary objective, no matter how it was achieved.

[43] See Rodell, 4-5.

[44] See Watson, 316. In 1953 a site of an iron foundry of the third century BCE was found in Xinglong County, Hebei Province. Large amounts of iron artifacts dating to the fourth century BCE have also been found. It is possible that the technique of iron smelting came to China from the West "through Scythian intermediaries, for contacts with the iron-using nomadic peoples of Siberia were sufficiently intense that independent invention was hardly possible." See Suzanne Young, et al., "The Earliest Use of Iron in China," *Metals in Antiquity* (Oxford: Archaeopress, 1999), 1-9.

[45] See Graff and Higham, 21.

[46] Richard F. Burton, *The Book of the Sword* (Mineola, NY: Dover Publications, 1987), 63. Sir Richard Francis Burton, a nineteenth century English explorer, soldier, and author has conducted detailed

studies tracing the origin and development of the sword while drawing from a variety of literal and archaeological sources. Although Burton provides a detailed and informative account of sword history, the text spans centuries and covers a wide range of cultures. With respect to Chinese swords and swordsmanship, Burton provides only piecemeal information about metallurgy and the sword as a weapon and symbol of courage and perfection.

[47] The Chinese were not alone in their ability to forge quality swords through pattern welding. Several other societies, including the Romans, Celts, Indians, Tibetans, and (later) Vikings relied on similar techniques.

[48] See Ko. Late Spring and Autumn or early Warring States period bronze jian of laminated construction were the ancestral prototype of the forge-welded/laminated sword seen later in the steel swords of the Han and Tang dynasties. See Thomas Chen, *Warring States and Qin Dynasty Swords*, http://thomaschen.freewebspace.com/custom4.html.

[49] The Zhou was invaded by nomads from the northwest as early as the Spring and Autumn period. Conflicts between nomadic people and settled Chinese would continue through much of China's history. See International Museum of the Horse, *Chinese History: A Brief Overview*, http://www.ket.org/artofthehorse/ed/hist.htm.

[50] See Burton, 127-131.

[51] See Rodell, 265-266. The tip of the jian was used mainly for a thrusting attack to soft tissue areas such as the throat, abdomen, or armpits. Before eliminating the opponent, however, one must neutralize the threat, which was done by attacking a

secondary target such as the arm. The swordsman could use the tip of the weapon by targeting the opponent's fingers or forearm. Even a shallow cut to the top of the forearm could sever the ligaments needed for controlling the thumb, making the opponent unable to grip his weapon.

[52] Ibid., 43-44. The femoral artery, the main blood vessel supplying blood to the leg, begins in the lower abdomen and extends through the thigh. Severing this blood vessel will result in heavy bleeding and possibly death, as will cuts to the femoral vein.

[53] See Zhang Yun, 90. By contrast, the European medieval longsword, which was also a straight weapon, commonly relied on heavy chopping moves rather than finesse.

[54] Ibid., 97-98.

[55] Ibid., 65-73.

[56] Ibid., 108-111.

[57] Ibid., 39-40.

[58] Zhuangzi, translated by Thomas Chen, China History Forum, http://www.chinahistoryforum.com/lofiversion/index.php/t8919.html.

[59] Chinese military treatises continued to emulate unpredictability—the essence of Sunzi's teachings—even after Sunzi's death, as demonstrated in the Han Dynasty work, *The Spring and Autumn Annals of Wu and Yueh*. See Chinese Archery, *The Spring and Autumn Annals of Wu and Yueh*, translated by Stephen Selby (Hong Kong: Hong Kong University Press, 2000), 156-157.

[60] See Rodell, 7 & 21.

[61] See Zhang Yun, 50-51.

[62] Lt. Col. Dave Grossman with Loren Christensen, *On Combat: The Psychology and Physiology of Deadly Conflict in War and in Peace* (Belleville, IL: PPCT Research Publications, 2004), 193.

[63] See Rodell, 12-13.

[64] Zhang Yun, 18.

[65] The Terra Cotta Army was buried with the first emperor of Qin around 210 BCE, and comprises more than 8,000 life-size figures of warriors and horses. The figures, constructed of pottery, carry real weapons.

[66] See Beale.

[67] Chinese Swords, *Chronology Table on 2500 Years of Chinese Sword Technical Developments*.

[68] See International Museum of the Horse.

[69] David A. Graff, *Medieval Chinese Warfare, 300-900* (New York, NY: Routledge, 2002), 41.

[70] See Graff and Higham, 27.

[71] See Rodell, 21-24. When comparing Chinese and European sword techniques, one finds that many of the maneuvers rely on common sense coupled with principles of physics. Several similarities exist despite the lack of contact between the geographical regions.

[72] See Zhang Yun, 80-81.

[73] Burton, 127.

[74] See Beale. There is little evidence of what type of swordsmanship existed in the Han Dynasty. Throughout Chinese history, pictorial representations of dao and finds from graves suggest that the dao was the more desirable weapon. The jian, however, continued to be carried in both military and civilian circles.

[75] A straight blade is effective for thrusting cuts, but less effective for slashing. If the swordsman desired to slash with a straight blade he must impact the target with as long a portion of the blade as possible, and draw the blade across the target and back toward himself. By contrast, a curved blade does not need to be drawn across the target. The curve, which is always presented at an angle to the target, will automatically produce an efficient cut even if the swordsman uses a chopping motion. A comparison can be made to the guillotine which chops straight down, yet effectively severs the head from the body. The efficient cut is a result of the slanted design of the blade.

[76] See Philip Tom and Thomas Chen, *An Introduction to Chinese Sabers: The Peidao of the Ming Through Qing Dynasties*, China History Forum, http://www.chinahistoryforum.com/lofiversion/index.php/t8919.html. The curved design of the saber is one reason why this weapon proved so useful in cavalry combat: The swordsman could strike while in motion without a great deal of precision, and still accomplish the objective.

[77] Graff, 41.

[78] It might be interesting to note that Roman infantry used short straight swords in order to achieve greater protection against an enemy's cuts. According to Sir Richard F. Burton, quoting Vegetius, Roman victories in walking infantry "were owing to the use of the point rather than the cut: When cutting, the right arm and flank are exposed, whereas during the thrust the body is guarded, and the adversary is wounded before he perceives it." See Burton, 127.

[79] See Beale.

[80]See Master Forge, *History of the Jian: Xia and Zhou Dynasty*, http://www.masterforge.co.uk/Jian%20Sword%20Collection.htm. Because the jian had two sharp edges, moves that required an edge to pass close to the body, and that could be done safely with the dao, would not be attempted with the jian. It is thus likely that this female sword master demonstrated her skills for the purpose of pleasing an audience, and not for the purpose of going into combat.

[81]See Rand, 109.

[82]See International Museum of the Horse.

[83]See Graff, 18.

[84]See Zhuge Liang, *The Way of the General*, translated by Thomas Cleary, http://kongming.net/novel/writings/wotg. Although *The Way of the General* provides timeless principles applicable to training the troops and winning their loyalty—for example, train soldiers without fail, train them in conduct and duty, awe them with rewards and punishments—this military treatise appears to be designed primarily for the training of mass armies and not for the education of single troops conducting edged weapon warfare. Moreover, it is general in scope and displays several similarities to the *Seven Military Classics of Ancient China*, in which Sunzi's *Art of War* is, perhaps, the best known of the ancient Chinese military sources. Note that in contrast to the scarcity of translated Asian sword treatises, Europe can provide several primary sources on western medieval swordsmanship; for example, *Hanko Döbringer's Fechtbuch* and *Master Sigmund Ringeck's Commentaries on Johann Liechtenauer's Fechtbuch*.

[85] Ibid.
[86] See Chin.
[87] See Rodell, xiv.
[88] See Rand, 107-137.
[89] See Ancient Edge, *Chinese Swords*, http://www.ancientedge.com/subcategory_34.html.
[90] See Rodell, 2.
[91] See Walther Heissig, "Tracing Some Mongol Oral Motifs in a Chinese Prosimetric Ming Novel of 1478," *Asian Folklore Studies*, Vol. 53, No. 2 (1994), 228-230. The story, which was found in 1967 when the grave of a Chinese noblewoman was excavated, portrays the hero Hua Guan Suo.
[92] Ibid, 231-243. According to the *Hua guan suo zhuan*, Guan Yu, Guan Suo's father, suffered defeat in battle and lost his sword into the deep water of a pond. When Guan Suo nearly died in battle, he had an experience of descending into hell where he was told that he must return for the sword if he were to win the victory. Following this call of duty, he recovered the renowned sword from the deep water of the pond.
[93] See Graff, 11.
[94] Albert Dien, *The Stirrup and Its Effect on Chinese Military History*, Silkroad Foundation, http://www.silk-road.com/artl/stirrup.shtml.
[95] Ibid.
[96] See Tom, "Some Notable Sabers of the Qing Dynasty at the Metropolitan Museum of Art," 207.
[97] See Thomas Chen, *Sui / Tang Sword and Fittings*, http://thomaschen.freewebspace.com/custom.html.
[98] Stephen V. Grancsay, "Two Chinese Swords Dating about A.D. 600," *The Metropolitan Museum*

of Art Bulletin, Vol., 25, No. 9 (Sep. 1930), 195. One of the straight swords discussed in this article is single edged; thus, not the typical jian. Translations from the mid-eighteenth century compendium of regulations, the *Huangchao Liqi Tushi*, further contribute to discussions about the controversy surrounding custom made swords and the exchange of swords across vast distances.

[99]Ibid., 194.

[100]See Sylvanarrow, *Ancient Medieval Weapons and Armor*, http://home.comcast.net/~sylvanarrow/jian.htm.

[101]See Seven Stars Trading Company, *Myths About Chinese Swordsmanship*, http://www.sevenstarstrading.com/articles/myths. The Seven Stars Trading Company, which specializes in antique Asian, Islamic, and Pacific arms and armor, examines some of the common myths about Chinese swordsmanship.

[102]See Grancsay, 194.

[103]See Rodell, 15-19.

[104]See Seven Stars Trading Company, *Myths About Chinese Swordsmanship*.

[105]See Rodell, 20-21.

[106]See Travel China Guide, *Sui Dynasty*, http://www.travelchinaguide.com/intro/history/sui. "Bad weather, internal divisions, and major Tang campaigns against [the Turks] eventually led to the submission of the Eastern Turks to the Tang in 630 [CE]." See Graff and Higham, 68.

[107]See Tom, *The Art of the Chinese Sword*. Also noteworthy is that China's cast iron industry produced cannon two hundred years prior to the same technological advances in the western world. Cannon

may have been the determining factor in China's victory over Japan during the invasion of the Korean peninsula in the 1590s, considered one of the seminal events in East Asian history. From Ken Swope's Lecture, *Changes & Continuities in Warfare, ca. 900-1500*, Norwich University, VT, 2006. However, China experienced no true "gunpowder revolution." On the battlefield, gunners served alongside of soldiers wielding swords, bows, and spears. Newer and older weapons were thus combined. Although firearms originated in China, they supplemented rather than replaced other types of weapons. See Graff and Higham, 28.

[108] Damascus steel blades were common also in Middle Eastern sword making from around 1100 CE. It is speculated that the technique derived its name from swords that were forged in Damascus, the capital and largest city of Syria. Damascene swords studied at museums have revealed that the Damascus pattern was "created by clusters of iron carbide, which show up as white against the dark steel . . . and were induced by repeated cycles of heating and cooling [until] impurities separate out, the ferric carbide particles congregating and growing around these impurities at each heating and cooling." See Richard Cohen, *By the Sword: A History of Gladiators, Musketeers, Samurai, Swashbucklers, and Olympic Champions* (New York, NY: Modern Library, 2002), 109.

[109] See Tom, *The Art of the Chinese Sword*.

[110] Ko.

[111] See Tom, "Some Notable Sabers of the Qing Dynasty at the Metropolitan Museum of Art," 214-216.

[112] See Chinese Swords, *Chronology Table on 2500 Years of Chinese Sword Technical Developments*.

[113] See Rand, 111-127. Compare this idea to the Japanese swordsman Yamamoto Tsunetomo's statement that a person who "has his sword out all the time . . . is habitually swinging a naked blade; people will not approach him and he will have no allies. If a sword is always sheathed, it will become rusty, the blade will dull, and people will think as much of its owner." See Yamamoto Tsunetomo, *Hagakure: The Book of the Samurai*, Chapter 2, http://split-kitty.com/misc/Hagakure.

[114] International Museum of the Horse.

[115] See Ko.

[116] See Chinese Swords, *The Chinese Sword Versus the Japanese Sword*, http://chineseswords.freewebspace.com/contact.html.

[117] Thomas Chen, *Song and Yuan Swords*, http://thomaschen.freewebspace.com/catalog.html.

[118] See Ko.

[119] Tom, "Some Notable Sabers of the Qing Dynasty at the Metropolitan Museum of Art," 207.

[120] The cross-draw was also used in other Asian and Islamic cultures, including Japan, Vietnam, the Ottoman Empire, and the Caucasus.

[121] Tom, *The Art of the Chinese Sword*.

[122] Tom, "Some Notable Sabers of the Qing Dynasty at the Metropolitan Museum of Art," 217. To demonstrate some differences in saber design, the goosequill saber of the Ming (1368-1644 CE) and middle Qing (1644-1912 CE) dynasties portrays a blade that is straight until the center of percussion (the desired point of impact which produces the least

amount of vibration in the blade), where the curve begins. The willow-leaf saber of the same period has a gentle curve throughout its length. The broad-bladed oxtail saber of the late Qing Dynasty was used by civilians and was not popular with the military. Today, this type of sword is called a Chinese broadsword. See Thomas Chen, *An Intro into Some Blade Types*, China History Forum, http://www.chinahistoryforum.com/lofiversion/index.php/t8919.html.

[123] See Thomas Chen, *Song and Yuan Swords*.

[124] See Thomas Chen, *Ming and Qing Swords*, credit given to research conducted by Philip Tom http://thomaschen.freewebspace.com/photo2.html.

[125] See Tom, "Some Notable Sabers of the Qing Dynasty at the Metropolitan Museum of Art," 209. The guard protected the hand against cuts. European swords commonly featured *quillons* projecting from the hilt between the tang and the blade. The quillons allowed one to hook an opponent's sword, should it slide down along one's own blade, and disarm him. Quillons were not common on Chinese swords.

[126] See Sylvanarrow.

[127] See Tom, "Some Notable Sabers of the Qing Dynasty at the Metropolitan Museum of Art," 214.

[128] See Zhang Yun, 43.

[129] See Chinese Swords, *The Chinese Sword Versus the Japanese Sword*.

[130] Superior Sword Company, *Chang Dao Sword History*, http://superiorsword.com/changdao_sword_history.htm.

[131] See Chinese Swordsmanship, *Portrait of Ming Dynasty General Qi Jiguang*, http://chineseswordsmanship.freewebspace.com/photo.html.

[132] See Ji Xiao Xin Shu, *General Qi's Military Manual*, http://chineseswords.freewebspace.com/contact.html.

[133] See Tom and Chen. Broadening tip areas were common also on Turkic sabers in the medieval period.

[134] See Paul Chen, *Chinese Weapons*, http://www.nihonzashi.com/ChineseWeapons.htm.

[135] Burton, 132.

[136] See Philip Tom, *The Art of the Chinese Sword*. The piece of hardened steel that was used to form the edge ran all the way through the body of the sword, appearing on both edges. This core was then sandwiched between walls of somewhat softer layered steel, which served as a support medium for the harder and more brittle central core. The ideal blade had a "very hard cutting edge backed by a softer blade body, which retain[ed] the resilience to absorb shock." Seven Stars Trading Company, *Myths About Chinese Swordsmanship*.

[137] Tom, "Some Notable Sabers of the Qing Dynasty at the Metropolitan Museum of Art," 210-214.

[138] See Chin. The style of the older battlefield tradition can be contrasted with the public style of swordsmanship, which focused on deflections and control of the opponent's weapon.

[139] See Tom, "Some Notable Sabers of the Qing Dynasty at the Metropolitan Museum of Art," 216.

[140] Tom and Chen.
[141] See Rodell, 44-45.
[142] See Franz H. Michael, "Chinese Military Tradition-II," *Far Eastern Survey*, Vol. 15, No. 6 (Mar. 27, 1946), 84-85.
[143] Ancient Edge. The broadsword was viewed as an instrument of combat that had the power to kill "whatever it touches." However, soldiers normally preferred lighter weapons that could be carried over long distances, and which were easier to wield in quick motions without tiring the swordsman prematurely. See Reg Penson, *The Chinese Broadsword*, http://www.chuanfa.co.uk/listings/10.html.
[144] See China View, "Light Shed on 1937 Lugouqiao Incident," *Xinhua News Agency* (2003), http://news.xinhuanet.com/english/205-07/07/content_3187424.htm. Although the Chinese understood the nuances of metallurgic science and employed sophisticated methods of sword making, they often won their battles through good logistics and organization coupled with the use of a multitude of weapons such as various forms of artillery, pikes, halberds, and swords. See Alex Huangfu, *Chinese Arms*, http://www.chinesearms.com.
[145] CCTV International, *Ancient Swords on Display in Guangzhou*, edited by Liu Fang, http://www.cctv.com/program/cultureexpress/20071108/102582.shtml.
[146] Graff, 21.
[147] Sawyer, 371.
[148] Ancient Edge.
[149] See Ko.

[150] See Chinese Swords, *The Chinese Sword Versus the Japanese Sword*.

[151] See Luó Guànzhōng, *Three Kingdoms*, translated by C. H. Brewitt-Taylor, http://www.threekingdoms.com. Three well-known heroes of China's past exemplify Chinese chivalry. These are Mulan of the Eastern Han (25-220 CE), Guan Yu of the Three Kingdoms period (220-263 CE), and Yue Fei of the Southern Song Dynasty (1127-1279 CE). See Rodell.

[152] See China Culture, *Yue Fei*, http://www.chinaculture.org/gb/en_madeinchina/2005-07/21/content_70831.htm.

[153] See Confucius Wisdoms, *Confucius*, http://www.geocities.com/Tokyo/Pagoda/6917/confuciu.html.

[154] See Sawyer, 155-156.

[155] CCTV International.

[156] Du Fu, *The Little Rain*, The Free Library, http://cranmer-byng.thefreelibrary.com/Lute-of-Jade/1-18.

BIBLIOGRAPHY

Ancient Edge. *Chinese Swords.* http://www.ancientedge.com/subcategory_34.html.

Bai Yunxiang. "Origin of Bronze and Iron in China." *Institute of Archaeology.* Beijing, China: Chinese Academy of Social Sciences, 2005.

Beale, Mark. *Terra Cotta Weapons: Weapons of Ancient China.* http://dana.ucc.nau.edu/msb46/Weapons_of_Ancient_China.html.

Burton, Richard F. *The Book of the Sword.* Mineola, NY: Dover Publications, 1987.

CCTV International. *Ancient Swords on Display in Guangzhou.* Edited by Liu Fang. http://www.cctv.com/program/cultureexpress/20071108/102582.shtml.

Chase, Kenneth. *Firearms: A Global History to 1700.* New York, NY: Cambridge University Press, 2003.

Chen, Thomas. *An Intro into Some Blade Types.* China History Forum, http://www.chinahistoryforum.com/lofiversion/index.php/t8919.html.

………*Ming and Qing Swords.* Credit given to research conducted by Philip Tom. http://thomaschen.freewebspace.com/photo2.html.

.........*Song and Yuan Swords.* http://thomaschen.freewebspace.com/catalog.html.

.........*Sui / Tang Sword and Fittings.* http://thomaschen.freewebspace.com/custom.html.

.........*Swordsmiths Ganjiang and Oyue.* http://thomaschen.freewebspace.com/custom2.html.

.........*Warring States and Qin Dynasty Swords.* http://thomaschen.freewebspace.com/custom4.html.

Chin, Alexander. Review of *Chinese Swordsmanship: The Yang Family Taiji Jian Tradition*, by Scott Rodell. Sword Forum International. http://swordforum.com/articles/css/chineseswordsmanship.php.

China Culture. *Yue Fei.* http://www.chinaculture.org/gb/en_madeinchina/2005-07/21/content_70831.htm.

China View. "Light Shed on 1937 Lugouqiao Incident." *Xinhua News Agency* (2003). http://news.xinhuanet.com/english/205-07/07/content_3187424.htm.

Chinese Archery. *The Spring and Autumn Annals of Wu and Yueh.* Translated by Stephen Selby. Hong Kong: Hong Kong University Press, 2000.

Chinese Cultural Studies. *The Mandate of Heaven: Selections from the Shu Jing.*

http://acc6.its.brooklyn.cuny.edu/~phalsall/texts/shu-jing.html.

Chinese Swords. *Chronology Table on 2500 Years of Chinese Sword Technical Developments.* http://chineseswords.freewebspace.com/about.html.

.........*The Chinese Sword Versus the Japanese Sword.*
http://chineseswords.freewebspace.com/contact.html.

Chinese Swordsmanship. *Portrait of Ming Dynasty General Qi Jiguang.* http://chineseswordsmanship.freewebspace.com/photo.html.

Cohen, Richard. *By the Sword: A History of Gladiators, Musketeers, Samurai, Swashbucklers, and Olympic Champions.* New York, NY: Modern Library, 2002.

Confucius Wisdoms. *Confucius.* http://www.geocities.com/Tokyo/Pagoda/6917/confuciu.html.

Dien, Albert. *The Stirrup and Its Effect on Chinese Military History.* Silkroad Foundation. http://www.silk-road.com/artl/stirrup.shtml.

Du Fu. *The Little Rain.* The Free Library. http://cranmer-byng.thefreelibrary.com/Lute-of-Jade/1-18.

Emperor Kangxi History. *Emperor of China – Qing Dynasty.* http://www.paulnoll.com/China/Money/I-money-choices-pic1.html.

Graff, David A. *Medieval Chinese Warfare, 300-900.* New York, NY: Routledge, 2002.

Graff, David A. and Higham, Robin. *A Military History of China.* Boulder, CO: Westview Press, 2002.

Grancsay, Stephen V. "Two Chinese Swords Dating about A.D. 600." *The Metropolitan Museum of Art Bulletin*, Vol., 25, No. 9 (Sep. 1930).

Grossman, Dave, Lt. Col. with Christensen Loren. *On Combat: The Psychology and Physiology of Deadly Conflict in War and in Peace.* Belleville, IL: PPCT Research Publications, 2004.

Hansford, S. Howard. Review of "Chinese Bronze Age Weapons: The Werner Jannings Collection in the Chinese National Palace Museum," by Max Loehr. *Bulletin of the School of Oriental and African Studies, University of London*, Vol. 19, No. 3 (1957).

Heissig, Walther. "Tracing Some Mongol Oral Motifs in a Chinese Prosimetric Ming Novel of 1478." *Asian Folklore Studies*, Vol. 53, No. 2 (1994).

Hwang, Jim. "A Swordsmith and His Legacy." *Taiwan Review* (Nov. 2001). http://taiwanreview.nat.gov.tw/site/Tr/ct.asp?xItem=672&CtNode=128.

International Museum of the Horse. *Chinese History: A Brief Overview.* http://www.ket.org/artofthehorse/ed/hist.htm.

Ji Xiao Xin Shu. *General Qi's Military Manual.* http://chineseswords.freewebspace.com/contact.html.

Ko, Adrian. *The Development of Swords Through the Ages.* http://www.arscives.com/gallery/en/fireandforge/development.htm.

Luó Guànzhōng. *Three Kingdoms.* Translated by C. H. Brewitt-Taylor. http://www.threekingdoms.com.

Master Forge. *History of the Jian: Xia and Zhou Dynasty.* http://www.masterforge.co.uk/Jian%20Sword%20Collection.htm.

Michael, Franz H. "Chinese Military Tradition-II." *Far Eastern Survey*, Vol. 15, No. 6 (Mar. 27, 1946).

Miyamoto Musashi. *Book of Five Rings.* Translated by Thomas Cleary. Boston, MA: Shambhala, 2005.

Murawiec, Laurent. "China's Grand Strategy is to Make War While Avoiding a Battle." *Armed Forces Journal* (Jul. 2007). http://www.armedforcesjournal.com/2005/11/1164221.

Paul, E. Jaiwant. *Arms and Armour: Traditional Weapons of India.* Singapore: Lustre Press, 2004.

Penson, Reg. *The Chinese Broadsword.* http://www.chuanfa.co.uk/listings/10.html.

Rand, Christopher C. "Li Ch'üan and Chinese Military Thought." *Harvard Journal of Asian Studies*, Vol. 39, No. 1 (Jun. 1979).

Rodell, Scott M. *Chinese Swordsmanship: The Yang Family Taiji Jian Tradition.* Annandale, VA: Seven Stars Books and Video, 2005.

Sawyer, Ralph and Sawzer, Mei-chün. *The Seven Military Classics of Ancient China* including the *Art of War.* Boulder, CO: Westview Press, 1993.

Seven Stars Trading Company. *Myths About Chinese Swordsmanship.* http://www.sevenstarstrading.com/articles/myths.

Superior Sword Company. *Chang Dao Sword History.* http://superiorsword.com/changdao_sword_history.htm.

Swope, Ken. Lecture. *Changes & Continuities in Warfare, ca. 900-1500.* Norwich University, VT, 2006.

Sylvanarrow. *Ancient Medieval Weapons and Armor.* http://home.comcast.net/~sylvanarrow/jian.htm.

Tom, Philip. "Some Notable Sabers of the Qing Dynasty at the Metropolitan Museum of Art." *Metropolitan Museum Journal,* Vol. 36 (2001).

.........*The Art of the Chinese Sword.* Fighting Arts. http://www.fightingarts.com/reading/article.php?id=1 28.

Tom, Philip and Chen, Thomas. *An Introduction to Chinese Sabers: The Peidao of the Ming Through Qing Dynasties.* China History Forum. http://www.chinahistoryforum.com/lofiversion/index.php/t8919.html.

Travel China Guide. *Sui Dynasty.* http://www.travelchinaguide.com/intro/history/sui.

Watson, William. Review of *Chinese Bronze Age Weapons: The Werner Jannings Collection in the Chinese National Palace Museum*, by Max Loehr. *The Burlington Magazine,* Vol. 99, No. 654 (Sep. 1957).

Wu Dingbo and Murphy, Patrick D. *Handbook of Chinese Popular Culture.* Westport, CT: Greenwood Publishing Group, 1994.

Yamamoto Tsunetomo. *Hagakure: The Book of the Samurai*, Chapter 2. http://split-kitty.com/misc/Hagakure.

Young, Suzanne, et al. "The Earliest Use of Iron in China." *Metals in Antiquity.* Oxford: Archaeopress, 1999.

Yu, Miles Maochun. Conversation with the author. Norwich University, VT, 2007.

Zhang Yun. *The Art of Chinese Swordsmanship.* Boston, MA: Weatherhill, 1998.

Zhuangzi. Translated by Herbert A. Giles, first published in 1889. Galileo Library. http://www.galileolibrary.com/ebooks/as07/chuangtzu_page_24.htm.

……… Translated by Thomas Chen. China History Forum. http://www.chinahistoryforum.com/lofiversion/index.php/t8919.html.

Zhuge Liang. *The Way of the General.* Translated by Thomas Cleary. http://kongming.net/novel/writings/wotg.

About the Author:

Martina Sprague has a Master of Arts Degree in Military History from Norwich University in Vermont. She is the author of numerous books about military and general history. For more information, please visit her Web site: www.modernfighter.com.